Bill Mann has coped with more than his fair share of change, trauma and tragedy. He narrowly survived the 7/7 London bombings in 2005, only to lose his wife to cancer a few years later. Bill has not only adapted to change, but learned how to embrace it and make it a positive force in his life.

This book is dedicated to my mother and father – everything I am and everything I have achieved is thanks to them.

This book is also dedicated to my wife, Sarah; and children, Emily, Alice, Ed, Will and Tom. Everything I do, I do for them.

Bill Mann

HOW TO KEEP CALM AND CARRY ON

A Survivor's Guide to Coping with Change,
Trauma and Tragedy

AUSTIN MACAULEY PUBLISHERS™

LONDON · CAMBRIDGE · NEW YORK · SHARJAH

A CIP catalogue record for this title is available from the British Library.

ISBN 9781528916639 (Paperback)
ISBN 9781528916646 (Hardback)
ISBN 9781528916653 (E-Book)

www.austinmacauley.com

First Published (2019)
Austin Macauley Publishers Ltd
25 Canada Square
Canary Wharf
London
E14 5LQ

Many thanks to Steve Bolton for first planting the idea of writing a book in my head. It may have been several years ago but this book is a direct result of his comments. I would also like to thank Steve for his continued support, encouragement and opportunities he has brought my way throughout the whole process. Steve is a highly exceptional mentor to those of us lucky enough to have the benefit of his advice and wisdom.

Thanks too to Neil Meldrum for his professional advice and guidance from the outset, and all the edits and corrections along the way. I had to pick his brains all the way through the creation of this book. His enthusiasm for this project and personal interest in the book were a great source of confidence to me.

I will be forever grateful that my wife, Sarah, not only believes in me, but also believed that I had the insight and wisdom to write this book. She supported me throughout, provided valuable input and observations on the content, and even created all of the graphics. Thank you.

Table of Contents

Preface

Being caught up in a terrorist bomb explosion is, thankfully, not something that many of us experience. The psychological impact of this type of trauma is something that many have struggled to cope with. Even battled hardened soldiers suffer from PTSD for years after this type of event. Many people do not recover, they cope, just.

For Bill Mann, on his way to work on 7th July 2005, this was a life changing moment. He was used to commuting to work and had swapped the risks of a long daily commute on a busy motorway to the relative safety of a train journey. None of us expect to be the victim of a terrorist bomb, but that is what happened to Bill that day. It is incredible that he found the strength to resume his daily commute only a few days later and refused to let the incident compromise his life, his plans, and his goals.

To deal with one such life changing event is an achievement, to get back up and carry on with life requires enormous inner strength. A few short years later his wife was diagnosed with terminal cancer and Bill was knocked down again. Only this time it was his family and his whole world that was rocked to its foundations. Undoubtedly, his earlier experience will have helped, but these two events, in quick succession, totally changed his life. Yet again, he got up and continued with his life, providing the stability, support, and strength his young family needed. It is a testament to his incredible inner strength that not only was he able to cope with these changes, but that he was able to successfully rebuild his life, and carry his family through the tragedy.

Bill spent many years on self-reflection, understanding the psychology of change, and developing the personal tools and techniques to help him cope. Ultimately, he learnt how to do more than cope, he learnt how to embrace change and turn it to his advantage. The knowledge and wisdom he shares in this book are of value to us all.

We all face change in our lives. Thankfully, not to the extremes that Bill has. But we all face changes as we go through life, changing jobs, moving house, embarking on new relationships, starting families, and so on. We all face change on an almost daily basis, our plans change, things happen, and we have to change course and accommodate them in our lives. The explanation of the change process that we go through, and the tools and techniques that Bill used, are applicable to all of us. This book is a fascinating and captivating journey through change. It makes us consider not only what we go through when facing change, but the impacts we have on others when we make change.

Looking back over the years, since Bill experienced these tragic events it is remarkable how he has come to accept them and used the experience to rebuild his life with extremely positive results. He has started not one, but two businesses, built a property portfolio and become financially independent, written a book, and become a thought leader in life change and lifestyle design. He is now in a position to share those experiences, and to help others that may not have the same insight. I thoroughly recommend the support he provides via this book and his mentoring services.

Steve Bolton.

Chapter One
Introduction

"Strength does not come from physical capacity. It comes from an indomitable will."

Mahatma Ghandi

It's the smells and sounds that stay with you. The taste of soot and smoke engulfed my senses for days, weeks and months afterwards. The sounds, of fear, distress, unimaginable pain and pure terror, became the soundtrack for my nightmares.

My name is Bill Mann and on July 7th 2005, I boarded a Circle Line London Underground train to Paddington. It was normal day for me. Balmy by the dubious standards of the English summer, so an uncomfortable commute lay ahead on London's bustling transport network, but my thoughts were on the day ahead. Meetings, specific jobs in the office in Paddington.

I'd said my usual goodbyes to my wife and children and set off for London Fenchurch Street, before wandering around the corner to Tower Hill underground station. I stood on the platform, in the same spot I always did despite the rush hour. When the train came to a screeching halt, I boarded the same carriage I always did. A creature of habit, perhaps, but perfect for a quick exit at the other end.

The train rolled into Edgware Road. I'd occasionally disembark there, and enjoy a walk into Paddington. I don't know why I didn't that day. If only I had.

I wouldn't describe myself as a people watcher on the Tube. Many are. Some are happy with their thoughts, like me, while others read the morning papers and most, in this digital age, are engrossed in their phones and tablets. I sat contemplating the day ahead as the train moved into the tunnel away from the Edgware Road platform.

A train passed beside us in the opposite direction as I was thrown from my seat towards the doors. The flash of light was blinding and the intensity of the heat scolded my skin which was already damp with sweat. The darkness was illuminated only by the emergency lighting in the tunnel and the burning embers that flashed past me. The screeching sound of metal on metal was only later drowned out by the screams that would haunt me.

They say your life flashes before you when you are so close to death and it is true. But a need to survive and pure instinct is what saved me that day, the day London had feared since the horrors of 9/11.

I waited for the impact that would surely end my life but it didn't come. The fireball that I thought would sweep through the carriage did not come. As the train ground to a halt, there was silence. After that, panic.

Fragments of broken glass showered down on me. I put out my hand and managed to grab a hand rail to break my fall. Slowly, as people surveyed the situation, all those able to started to help the injured and the dying. Passengers in the passing train looked through their windows in horror. Some broke windows and passed in bottles or water or climbed through to help. Some people had been blown out of the carriage by the force of the bomb and others jumped down to help them.

The evacuation had started but I stayed to help. The emergency services arrived faced with their worst nightmare, and I will never forget the words of the paramedic that first walked through and assessed the situation with his colleagues: "Five fatalities and five seriously injured."

I was one of the lucky ones that was able to walk out the carriage unaided. Shock cripples you in the moments when you need your strength most; I struggled to walk to the end of the train and down a ladder on to the tracks and out of the station.

The man that emerged into the warm air of North London was very different to the one that had boarded the train just minutes earlier. My life had changed in an instant. My priorities were turned upside down and my perspective permanently changed. For a moment the only thing that mattered was life over death. The thoughts that had dominated my morning were redundant. Thoughts of the things I had to do at work vanished. Thoughts of other things that were once important vanished into the background. Bills to pay, the mortgage, house to renovate, cars to run, job security. They suddenly became unworthy of the worry and stress that they once taken. Life and health were the only need, and still are.

Outside of the station we were shepherded into the local branch of Marks & Spencer where staff were providing chairs and water, before we were moved over the road to the Hilton Metropole Hotel where ambulance staff and paramedics assessed the injured. Being one of the least injured, I was in the final tranche of people taken to the Royal Free Hospital in Hampstead.

Although covered in blood from people I had tried to assist, my only physical injury was blast damage to my eardrums and a few minor cuts and scratches. I was rather bemused when the doctor said I was free to go home. I was on the wrong side of London, and the whole transport network was shut down.

Eventually, I was able to find a mini-cab. The driver was an immigrant from Afghanistan that had lost several family members in similar circumstances. He was one of the few people I have spoken to that has any understanding of the trauma. Eventually, I made it home. The house was empty, and I showered off the blood and grime. I showered again to get clean, but didn't feel it. My clothes went straight into a black sack and were put outside the back door. The children walked in from school later that afternoon and wondered why their dad was home early from work.

Such a profound change took years to adjust to and to accept. This was a major trauma that only others that had been through a similar event could comprehend. Indeed, it was only when I met a victim of a similar terrorist bombing that I was able to move forward. It was a trauma that I largely had to deal with myself as others could not relate to. The questions were endless. Why? Why me? What if I had sat a few seats further up? What if I had entered a different set of doors? Why that train and not the one earlier or later? What if I had got off at Edgware Road? So many questions but no answers. What next? Do I go back to work and do that journey again every day? Do I let it change my life by having to change job and not commute? Why should it? Why should I let the terrorists win? More and more questions. Fewer and fewer answers.

I decided I had to get back in the saddle and do the journey again and not be defeated. I could not give up a good job. I could not stop visiting London when I lived on its doorstep. I could not have my life compromised so severely. The decision was not just a practical one. It was a choice of falling to pieces or facing up to reality and getting on with life. I felt on the edge – I could easily have gone either way. In the days and weeks that followed more and more individual stories came out and I could understand and sympathise with them all.

Going back to work, I had very refreshing clarity regarding my inbox and to-do list. None of it was of any consequence. Not to say that none of it was important, or even that others would not view it as extremely important or critical to the business. My frame of reference had changed. Never before had the value of life been so profound, or the fragility of life been so scary. Every day was something to give thanks for and every day was an opportunity to cherish and take advantage of. This new perspective was both a blessing and a curse. How could I be motivated by a presentation deck to be delivered to a committee for approval? How could I consider writing a report as a good use of the precious hours I had in my day? Motivation to make the most of each and every day was very strong and something I have tried to retain. Motivation to deal with things of little or no consequence against my new frame of reference was a struggle.

I felt I was just getting my head above water and coming to terms with what happened when my wife, my life partner since we were both 17, was diagnosed with cancer. A few years later, it returned, and this time it was terminal. This time it was not just myself but our children I had to help through this tragedy.

Yet again my life, our life, was turned upside down. Perspectives changed, priorities changed, and our futures changed. Without doubt my experience of dealing with the personal impacts of surviving the bomb helped me get through this period. I knew the mental strength was there that I could draw on. I knew the self-defence mechanisms were there that I could rely on. I knew I had the tools and techniques to help me cope and process this most drastic and brutal change to our lives. It is not without pride that I look back at how successful this has been, and how I have been able to guide the children through it, to become happy and well balanced young adults. It could have been so different.

Before both of these events, and since then, there have been other changes I have had to face that are far more common. Both positive and negative, planned and unexpected. The sort of changes that many people face during their lives: starting a new job, losing a job, moving house, starting relationships, having children, ending relationships, and so on. We all face change on a day-to-day basis. Events change our plans for the days or weeks ahead, whether it be a cancelled appointment, travel delays, unexpected visitors, etc. All of these things are a change and they can all invoke the same set of emotions and turmoil, albeit on a smaller scale. How many people get frustrated or even angry if their plans for the day are changed, even if it cannot be helped? Sometimes, these minor daily irritations can change our outlook on the whole day or even longer. They all require us to process the change and make decisions about how we move forward. The scale may be different but it is fundamentally the same process we go through.

I am not here to judge, nor to say my experience of 7/7 and my wife's death mean those, whose plans have been ruined simply don't match up to what I have been through. Far from it, change is relative and how you deal with it can make you or break you, regardless of the scale of the event.

My earlier experiences have certainly helped me keep those smaller scale changes in perspective and allowed me to accept and adapt to them much easier than I would have in the past. But even looking back before the bomb I can recognise in myself an ability to keep a cool head in the face of change and not be phased by events that others struggle with, the ability to 'Keep Calm and Carry On'.

In this book I will draw out the tools and techniques I have used successfully to process change. Whether it be the major trauma and tragedy of the events I have described above or less significant change that can occur in all our lives daily. I will describe the psychology of change and models for change. Most importantly, I will show you how the tools and techniques I have used can be applied to many different types of change and, ultimately, help you accept change and move forward.

I will also look at what change is and how, in almost every case, there are opportunities and positive effects to take from it. Even in the bleakest of circumstances there can ultimately be a positive outcome. Conversely, with positive and planned change there is often negative unforeseen consequences. Change is change – there are positive and negative implications. When dealing with change it is important to recognise this to separate emotion from objective assessment. I will show how doing this allows you to make better decisions and make the most out of each situation.

Finally, I will look at the practicalities of planned and unplanned changes. We all know the unexpected can happen, so why are we unprepared? We take action after an event has happened. After the 7/7 bombs, commuters on the London Underground were openly more guarded and aware of their surroundings. After losing a job we make sure we have income protection insurance in the future. After being caught by a speed camera we (most of us) take more care. We cannot plan or insure for every eventuality but my experiences have shown just how tenuous life can be. Opportunities need to be taken when they arise without fearing change. Similarly, the things that can threaten our livelihoods, our lifestyles, or even our lives can sometimes be negated to avoid the unwanted change.

By the end of this book, you will have a better understanding of what change is, how to process and accept it, to not fear change but to embrace the opportunities it brings with confidence. You will know how to 'Keep Calm and Carry On'.

Chapter Two
What Is Change?

"Change is the only constant in life."

Heraclitus

The examples I have given in the introduction – a personal trauma and loss of a loved one at an early age are both obvious examples of life changing events. Many people, but thankfully only a minority, go through similar experiences.

Most people will encounter other major changes in life, however. This could be moving house, changing job, losing a job, starting a relationship, ending a relationship, starting a family, an injury or illness, and so on. All of these things have an impact on the lives of the people involved.

Less significant change also happens to us all far more frequently, almost daily. But its lesser significance does not make it any less paralysing for the individual or individuals involved. Organisational changes in the workplace are a regular occurrence. Working and playing with new teams at work or at home is a change. As is starting a new hobby or joining a course.

Career, business, social and leisure opportunities arise all the time, leading to a change in direction. All of these things have an impact on our lives and are a change to be accepted. Change also happens to us at a very low level every day. Traffic jams can result in a missed appointment, often giving rise to the full range of emotions of major change. Cancelled meetings, unexpected visitors, an appliance breaking down, unexpected bills or fines, the car not starting, a power cut, and so on. All of these things result in a change to how we expected our day to unfold, and sometimes they can all be difficult to process and accept. They can all be frustrating, disappointing, and cause us to look at our options and replan our day. Change is all around us and a daily occurrence. Change really is the only constant in life.

Planned and Unexpected

Not all change is unexpected and forced upon us. Moving house or changing job is planned. Joining a course or sports team is planned. All of these things and many other planned events can have an impact on your life and result in change. Just because it is planned, it does not mean it is easier to process and accept. We enter this change with certain expectations and when the reality is different, this impacts us as change.

With unexpected change, by definition, our immediate days, weeks, and months ahead are altered. Our expectations are unfulfilled. We have lost the vision of how those days, weeks, and months were going to unfold. Regardless of how welcome or not the change is, our expectations are dashed.

It can be a similar experience with planned change. When we plan a major change like moving house or starting a new job we have an expectation of what life will be like afterwards. The greater the change, the greater emphasis we give that expectation. More often than not the reality is different. Not necessarily worse or better – just different. That difference is where the personal change arises and where challenges exist in accepting it. For example, when starting a new job this will have been planned for several months in advance and we will have high expectations of the job and career opportunities. However, often the reality will be different. There are new relationships to be built, expectations on performance to be met, and issues in getting the job done to be overcome. This is a planned change that will take several months to adapt to.

Positive and Negative

Whether it is planned or not, change is often perceived as positive or negative in the first instance. More accurately, it will have a combination of positive and negative aspects but overwhelmingly the first instinct will be to view the change as either good or bad.

A lottery win is unplanned but considered a positive change. However, although positive it could be a life-changing event. It may also bring with it a number of negative aspects such as unwelcome publicity and so on. Both the positive and negative aspects of the change will result in a range of emotions and challenges in accepting the change. Pregnancy is often unplanned and usually considered good news, although not always. Again it is a life-changing event and may well have implications that are considered negative, such as maternity leave and financial change. Being offered a promotion is often unexpected but is also a change that has to be adapted to. There are many examples of unplanned changes that can be viewed as positive. However, they have an impact on our lives which we have to understand and accept. Adapting to the change will include both challenges and opportunities, and generate a range of emotions.

Similarly, there are many examples of planned changes that become a negative experience. The new job can rapidly become a major disappointment. Starting a new job will be planned and considered positive. The reality may be a difficult new boss, or challenging targets, or other unforeseen challenges. Starting a new activity, such as joining a gym, is planned and associated with positive expectations for fitness and health. The reality is often different. In addition to the physical challenges, the emotional challenges of making the change in lifestyle are equally demanding. A planned change, even if made for all the right reasons, can become very difficult to make. It will also consist of many challenges and opportunities, and will also generate a range of emotions.

Scale of Change

The process and challenges of accepting change apply not just to major trauma or incidents. The process applies equally to minor small scale changes such as those we face on a daily basis. In this case dealing with the change may be much quicker but not always. The impact and effects of change may be minor but the process of dealing with it will be similar.

As an example, consider discovering a flat tyre on your car. The immediate reaction will be one of shock or surprise. This will be quickly followed by a consideration of the consequences. The immediate concern, perhaps, focuses on the cost of repair, or the delay in getting home or to work, or it may just be the practicalities of getting it fixed. Depending on the circumstances, this will lead to a range of emotions. It may be worry over the cost, frustration or anger at a missed appointment, or even complete ambivalence, if time and cost are of no concern, or you run a tyre replacement business!

You will then need to consider your options for getting the tyre repaired, paying for it, and rescheduling your day. All of these things may give rise to a different set of emotions, for example relief at sorting the problem out. At that point you can then make decisions and put them into action. Having done so, you have largely dealt with the change to your day and will probably feel the emotions subsiding. You now have a new plan for your day and a different set of expectations. The process you have been through and the range of emotions you have experienced are similar to that of a much more significant change, just on a smaller scale.

Understanding what happens, when faced with these minor changes, and why they lead to the emotions they do, can help keep those emotions in check. Often peoples' reactions are considered out of all proportion with the scale of the change or problem they are facing. By asking 'why' and understanding the process of change it is easier to control those emotions.

Reactions and Responses

When a trigger event or situation arises, it often feels like our immediate response is an emotional one. However, this is preceded by our thoughts and interpretation of the event and situation. We almost instantly jump to a conclusion regarding the impact of the event and its consequences. This then leads to our emotional response as shown in the diagram below. This usually happens so quickly that our emotions become tightly coupled to the (change) event itself and we associate one with the other.

Situation	Thought	Emotion	Behaviour
Something happens	Situation is interpreted	A feeling occurs as a result of the thought	An action in response to the emotion

Trigger-Response Process

We will often then take action as a result of our emotions, even if that is not the best time to decide how to react and proceed. Depending on the action we take, it may change the situation or lead to another event or situation. This in turn will lead to another reaction and potentially a whole cycle of events.

To use the flat tyre example: The trigger event is discovering the flat tyre. The immediate thought may be the inconvenience and impact to plans. This may be arriving late for work, or for collecting children from school. This in turn could lead to thoughts of worry and panic. In this state the action may not be the best option – for example taking a high interest short-term loan to fix the tyre. The initial trigger event has been addressed, but now there is a new situation: an unexpected and expensive debt. This cycle is sometimes referred to as the 'think feel do' cycle, as shown in the following diagram.

Think Feel Do Cycle.

A single trigger event may lead to several different reactions and responses which ripple across different parts of our lives. By distinguishing between the change event and our reactions and responses, it is easier to manage the change.

Change really is something we encounter all the time. It may be something we have planned or be completely unexpected. It may be something we consider as positive and good news, or something negative. It could be something minor that we deal with during our day, or over a few days and weeks. Or it could be something far more significant that could take months or years to accept.

Chapter Three
The Change Curve

"Change is hard at first, messy in the middle, and gorgeous at the end."

Robin Sharma

This chapter is not intended to be a theoretical discussion on change or an analysis of the psychology of change. There are many text books and other resources in existence that can provide a much more rigorous description. However, it is not possible to understand change, and therefore how to manage its effects, without a basic knowledge of how we react and respond to change, the emotions it generates, and why.

No discussion on change is complete without including the change curve which is probably the most well-known model. There are now many variations but the original model is attributed to Elisabeth Kubler-Ross. She first studied the impact of grief upon those who were dying or had just lost a loved one in the 1960s. Many types of change, particularly negative change, involve the loss of something such as a job or a partner, for example. This loss also creates a sense of grief or grieving in those that have suffered the loss. It also applies to change on a smaller scale. For example, if a holiday is cancelled we 'grieve' for what we have lost. It may be less significant and a shorter process but the model still applies. The model has since been developed and is now recognised to apply to many types of change. There are other models for change but for the purposes of this book we will use this one.

The change curve should not be read as linear progression. People move backwards and forwards through different emotions and progression is not as smooth as a curve suggests. The different variations may use different labels but all show the three distinct stages of the curve.

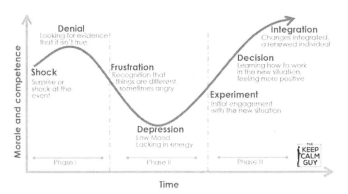

Change Curve

Stage 1: Shock and Denial

Shock

The first reaction to a trigger event. This does not always refer to a negative event and could equally be surprise at a positive event. The shock or surprise may also be felt when an event is partially or even fully expected. For example, even if redundancies are expected the moment of actually losing a job will trigger an emotional reaction. That the event itself has taken place can generate this emotion and is often due to the timing being out of the control of the individual. It may be short-lived or not. Shock, on a much smaller scale, also applies to more trivial changes. In the flat tyre example given previously, when this is discovered there is a sense of shock at this unexpected turn of events. It may be a short lived emotion but it is still the first step of processing the change.

Shock is often accompanied by confusion and disbelief. When the event is totally unexpected it raises numerous questions. Questions that the mind seeks answers for to make sense of what has happened. At this point the mind may jump to the wrong answer or wrong conclusion.

Denial

Particularly with negative change it is human nature to cling to the past, with what was known, and probably comfortable. Denial looks for possibilities to avoid the change or even evidence that the trigger event is not true or could be undone. By definition it is a lack of acceptance and rejection of the event. For example, the speeding ticket arriving in the post. The first instinct is to question whether it is correct, even with photographic evidence. We check it and double check it looking for some evidence that it is wrong. At the back of our mind our rational brain knows that it is correct.

We deny the change because our first instinct is to look for a way out of having to accept the change. If we can find a reason that the change may be 'wrong' or for negating it then we will. In extreme cases people will continue to look for reason even when none exist. The other reason we deny change is because we are not ready to face the alternative – the change is real and we have to face the consequences.

Stage 2: Anger/Frustration and Depression

Anger and Frustration

Frustration and even anger arise at the point where denial cannot continue. The realisation hits and the consequences of the change are faced. At this point we look for someone or something to blame. A target for our anger and frustration. We look at all the ways the change could have been avoided and ask 'why did you not'? At this point our rational brain knows that the question is pointless and the change cannot be undone. The temptation is to pick the easiest or most obvious target for our emotions. If we cannot find anybody else then we will often blame ourselves for being in the situation and think 'I should have…', or 'if only I had…'

Depression

As the frustration and anger fade away what is left is the absolute realisation of the change and its consequences. This is the lowest point, emotionally, when what has been lost must be faced. Focus is on the negative impact of the change. Not just what has been lost but also all the negative implications. Every minor point or irritation just adds to the sadness and depression.

This lowest point is also the turning point, although people do move backward and forward through the curve. We will start to acknowledge our options for moving forward no matter how briefly. It may be the consequences of this that pull us back into depression phase until we are ready to give them more consideration.

Stage 3: Experiment, Decision, Integration

Experiment

At this point we start to move forwards towards acceptance. We look at ways to deal with the change. We look for options to work with the change and mitigate the consequences. For example, when a job is lost we look at other options and possibilities. With the speeding ticket example, we look for options to reduce the fine with early payment. There are often options and opportunities that we start to identify and explore. We start to feel positive about the possibilities. The more action we take the more in control we feel. Our rational brain starts to take over from the emotion and look at the change and its implications with clearer thinking.

Decision

We are now able to take action and steps to deal with the change. We may still feel regret that the change has occurred but we recognise that it has happened and we have to move forward. As we take these steps we have a greater feeling of control and with control we feel more positive about the future. As we explore possibilities and opportunities we are able to identify positive aspects and as we do so we move towards acceptance.

Integration

Finally, we reach a point of acceptance and the change becomes integrated in our lives. We have accepted the change, taken action to address it and dealt with the consequences, and reached a new 'normal'. Emotions will have subsided and our expectations become realigned with the change.

At this point, if not earlier, we may identify other changes that are now soaking up our time and energy. Our focus and emotional energy will be diverted into other areas of our lives. As we come to accept the previous change we create, the emotional bandwidth to deal with other things – positive and negative. This is an indication that we have reached this stage in the change curve.

It is quite likely that the other events in our lives that are now demanding our attention are other types of change, or other events that lead to change. We often move from one change to another, deal with one change only to face another. In reality we are not dealing with one change in isolation, we are dealing with a series of changes of different types and different scale.

Applying It in Practice

The theory is one thing but how does this work in practice? The first thing to note is that the time an individual may spend at each stage will vary enormously. It depends on many factors. This is not just the scale of change and the impact, but is also everything else that is going on in the life of the person affected. Shock or disbelief may last seconds or months, frustration and anger may last a day or years. Similarly, the length of time each stage lasts has no relation to the length of time that the other stages will last. There are some important questions to ask when considering the timing. 'Am I spending too long dwelling or indulging in this stage'? It may be that you cannot help or control it but if so then ask, 'Why'? If you cannot find the answer, then ask, 'Do I need professional help to move on from this stage'?

Tip: Do not let others judge the timing or even answer the questions. They have not walked into your shoes.

The physical shock of the 7/7 bomb only stayed with me for minutes. As I left the train, I started to shake and struggled to walk down the carriage, but as soon as I was out of the train and walking away down the tracks it started to ease. By the time I was out of the station and in fresh air I could walk okay.

The emotional shock stayed with me for days and probably weeks or months. But the disbelief of what had happened lasted just seconds. The evidence was all around and was overwhelming. It was 24-hour news coverage on every channel. The reality of standing up in the carriage was real, gritty, and bloody.

The most critical aspect when considering the change curve in practice is that it is not linear. It is not a progression from one stage to the next and then to the end of the curve. People will move backwards and forwards between the steps in the curve and stages, often many times. People may seemingly skip over some steps or spend a long time on others. It is not a smooth progression through the curve.

Thoughts at one step can give rise to a new set of emotions or reignite old ones. This can push you backwards or forwards. For example, considering your options for the way forward can generate frustration and anger at how limited they are or the consequences that you have to face. This frustration and anger can take you right back to the start of the curve, and your frustration and anger that the change happened in the first place. Alternatively, at your lowest point someone may point out an opportunity you had not previously seen and you may suddenly start to feel more positive and able to move forward. The progression through the curve is unique and individual to each of us.

Tip: Your emotions are allowed. Give yourself permission to feel them. You do not need anyone-else's permission.

The Art of Self-Defence

Moving through the change curve is an emotional roller-coaster. With minor changes it may be an easy ride but with major life changes it may be a white-knuckle journey. Emotional extremes are mentally and physically exhausting. Defending against the mental and physical challenges of processing change can and does make a significant difference in progressing through the curve. In dealing with the trauma of the 7/7 bomb, and the tragedy of losing my wife, I adopted a number of techniques that I justified as self-defence.

Sleep

It is difficult to cope with the practicalities of change and the drain on emotions when tired. It is well documented that our performance in many areas of life is affected when we are tired or exhausted. By recognising this and giving ourselves enough time to sleep we are better able to deal with change. This can mean prioritising sleep over things that can wait until tomorrow. Giving sleep and rest sufficient priority is not a sign of weakness or procrastination. It is a pro-active choice and shows that you are taking control of the situation.

Note: Anyone not able to sleep when tired and given the time, due to stress or any other reason, especially if this continues for a prolonged period should seek medical advice.

It is important to recognise when we are tired and need rest. This is not the time to answer difficult questions or make significant decisions. The sub-conscious mind can work on these for you while you rest.

Tip: Defer answering questions or making decisions until you have rested. If they can wait, then let them.

Just Say No

Coping with major change sometimes means you have to put yourself first. This may seem selfish and sometimes it will be. Only you can judge when this is appropriate and necessary. It may be a task you are asked to do or even an offer of help from a well-meaning friend or relative that is going to take your time and effort. The critical factor is whether it will put more pressure on you at a time when you do not need it. If it is a request or offer that is going to increase that pressure rather than decrease it then it is a candidate for saying 'no' and politely refusing.

Tip: Question whether the task or offer of help is going to add to your pressures. If so, then politely declining or deferring may be the best option.

The question above may lead to another one: Are the people around you having a positive impact on you and the changes you are facing, or a negative one? Are they positive and supportive or negative and under-mining your confidence? Are they enabling you to move on or holding you back? Depending on how great the change and the challenges of adapting it may become advisable or even necessary to spend time differently. Seek out those that can help.

Asking for Help

Asking for help can take many forms. We do not like to ask for help directly for many reasons. It can seem a sign of weakness or being unable to cope. We prefer to be independent and our pride is hurt by simply stating we need help.

The challenges we face no matter how small or how large will have been faced by many people before us. Why not benefit from their knowledge and experience? It is the smart thing to do. Often, our struggles are due to a lack of information or advice that is available if we look for it. Indeed, the struggle itself is often a sign that input from others is needed. In the business environment, this is considered networking and building on the knowledge of others. It is considered a strength to be able to do this, compared with those who try to deal with things alone. It applies equally well to others aspects of our lives, and the input and support from others could provide the missing information that makes all the difference.

Tip: If something is a struggle and seems too hard then you do not have all the information you need to deal with it. Find someone who has.

Being Direct

This is no time to worry about being polite or diplomatic. In vagueness and lack of clarity is uncertainty and confusion. Whether saying 'no' or asking for assistance or advice clear communication is critical. Our fear of offending people is often misplaced. Clarity is welcomed. It avoids ambiguities and sets clear expectations. Our concern for politeness and not offending others takes time and effort as well as emotional energy. This energy may not be available or best reserved for dealing with the change itself. Preserve it.

One Step at a Time

Change and the implications and consequences of change can often seem daunting. Our instinct is to look at the whole picture and the magnitude of this can seem overwhelming.

This applies equally to the smaller changes and challenges we face on a day-to-day basis as well as the larger traumas and tragedies we can face in life. Depending on the scale of change it may take hours or days to process. Alternatively, it may take weeks, months, or even years. Ultimately, we can only deal with the challenges immediately in front of us and we need to break this into chunks that we can cope with.

In 2011, when the Oncologist told my family and I, there was nothing more he could do for my wife, our only way of coping was to take each day as it came. There was little value in planning for tomorrow because we did not know what it would bring. Each day was a struggle and our focus was the here and now. We had expectations for the coming days and weeks but actually they were in the future. There was little we could do to change what the future held but we could make today more comfortable. Sometimes, when even this was too much the focus became the next hour or two. The horizon came forward so that what we faced was something we could cope with.

Tip: When the mountain you are facing looks too great, focus on the next step and only the next step.

Taking Time

Last but not least, adapting to change takes time. By understanding the change curve, and where you are in it, you can gain perspective. This is particularly true in the early stages and in the 'dip' of the curve. While the desire is often to reach the end of the curve, the timing cannot be controlled. Trying to do so will create a false pressure that exacerbates the situation (see 'Just Say No' above). The time required will depend on the magnitude of the change and the impact on your life. Give yourself the freedom of time. The critical point about this technique for self-defence is that you *will* reach the end of the change curve. No matter how unlikely it seems and how difficult to believe when you are in stage two, you will reach the end of the curve.

Scale Examples

The change curve was originally identified to explain the process that people who are grieving go through. It is easy to see how this applies to people that are going through major life changing events such as losing a loved one, or the experience of a terrorist bomb in my case. Similarly, with other major events such as divorce or the break-up of a relationship. The range of emotions and journey through the change curve is something that many people will be able to identify with.

With smaller scale change, the curve is equally valid and also applicable. Let us use the example of a broken down appliance such as a washing machine. The initial reaction will be 'shock' that the machine is not working when we go to use it, we will be frustrated that we could not do the laundry as we had planned and expected, and then may be briefly 'depressed' that we are going to have the problem for some time until it is repaired or replaced. We will consider our options, make our decisions, and then accept what has happened and move on. In this case, we were grieving for a loss – a functioning washing machine, and went through the same process. This may have been a minor inconvenience to us and a simple change to process. However, if we were already in a difficult or stressful situation, such as having a large family to cater for, and perhaps little money to replace or repair the machine, then the emotions of the change curve and the implications of the change could be much more extreme.

Separating Emotions and Thoughts

As we move through the change curve, and attempt to deal with the change we face, then we experience a range of

36

emotions as described above. These can range from very negative emotions such as shock, anger, and depression, to positive ones such as hope, satisfaction, and achievement. We have many decisions to make as we go through the change curve. These can be internal decisions (in our own mind) about how think about what has happened, the options, and consequences, or practical ones about the actions we need to take as a result of the change. To make these decisions we need to separate our emotions from our rational thoughts. We need to make the decisions while we are being objective and reasoned. It may be tempting to act quickly in the heat of the moment, but unless in the face of danger, this is very rarely a good time to be making decisions.

Chapter Four
Managing Emotions

"Managing your impulsive, emotional chimp as an adult will be one of the biggest factors determining how successful you are in life."

Dr Steve Peters.

The challenges of dealing with change, such as a life-changing trauma or tragedy, are usually associated with the strength and depth of emotions that go with it. This applies to all change – even small-scale change can generate feelings of shock, surprise, anger, joy, etc.

It may not be the strength of feeling, but alternating between feelings that poses the biggest challenge. Or, perhaps, being stuck with a certain feeling for too long. These extremes of emotion can sap energy and people become worn down by the emotional drain. Things can be said while in an emotional state that are later regretted and decisions can be taken for the wrong reasons. Managing your emotions is an essential part of processing change.

This does not mean denying your emotions or refusing to express them, simply being aware of your emotions and not letting them become out of control.

Managing your own emotions gives rise to several questions:

- Why manage your emotions?
- They are natural, why not let them run free?

- Is there a time for controlling them?
- Is there a time for not?
- What is the 'problem' with emotions?

This chapter will answer those questions in the context of coping with change. Of course there is not a problem with expressing emotions (in general). They are part of who we are and part of our identity. But that is just the point – they stem from our brain and our thinking. They are not separate. People describe emotions as coming from the heart. That is simply a figure of speech. Our emotions arise from the way our brain processes information and, if left unchecked, emotion will influence our decisions and behaviours often in conflict with our adult rational brain. They will influence our lives perhaps in ways that our adult brain will later regret.

When we are overcome with an emotion, any emotion – positive or negative – we need to be aware that is the case. We need to be self-aware enough to know to be careful with our reactions and responses. We have all said or done things in the heat of the moment that later we regret. We may have deliberately said something hurtful just because we are angry, or we may have made a rash promise just because we are feeling excited by something. If we can be aware that we are being gripped by emotion, then we may be able to walk away from a situation and avoid these risks. It is much better to return when the emotion has subsided and our adult rational brain is back in charge. Similarly, this is not the time to make decisions of any consequence. If we do, then we are making decisions based on feelings rather than thoughts, and often on impulse rather than by design.

The quote on the previous page is from Dr Steve Peters and his excellent book The Chimp Paradox, and I recommend it to those striving for a much greater understanding of how the emotional (chimp) side of the brain works with the rational (adult) side of the brain. I will summarise the analogy below and put it in the context of managing change.

The brain is an incredibly complex organ that we still do not fully understand. It is a greatly simplified model but for the purposes of this chapter let us consider three elements:

1. The emotional part of our brain (the chimp).
2. The adult rational part of our brain.
3. Memory – Our reference library that both the adult and chimp refer back to.

When we encounter an event or situation our brain (chimp and adult) will try to interpret it and make sense of it by consulting our memory. Have we encountered this before? What happened? Was it a good experience or bad? What were the consequences? How does this relate to our new situation? Against this frame of reference we will make a judgement about this new event.

For example, someone facing redundancy for the second or third time will compare it with their previous experience. If the redundancy payment was a welcome bonus and another job was easy to come by they will interpret it one way. On the other hand, if the past redundancy led to financial hardship and a long period of unemployment they will look at differently. It may be that they have not encountered redundancy before but they will still consult their memory and reference all the times they have heard others speak of redundancy or stories they have read. This will inform their view of the current situation and they will respond accordingly. The same process applies to all change. Even with trivial examples we will refer back to our memory and past experiences and that will frame our response. Many people dread a buff coloured envelope arriving in the post because it usually contains an invoice. This is because our past experience of such envelopes is mainly negative. Rationally, we know the envelope could contain anything, and even be good news such as a refund, but the emotional part of our brain (the chimp) jumps in first.

Our chimp is first to respond – simply because it is quicker and stronger. It will respond before our adult brain is able to take over and deal with the situation. What happens next depends on how much freedom our chimp has and our ability to control it. It also depends on the scale and significance of the change.

Let us look at the two examples above. If we are given a redundancy notice at work, then we immediately think back to what we know about redundancy, jump to a conclusion, and we will respond with feelings. It could be feelings of fear, despondency, relief, or even pleasure. This is because our chimp has jumped in and responded to the trigger event. We will continue to express these emotions for as long as we want or need to vent. We need to release the emotions. Our adult brain has not yet had an opportunity to look at the options and opportunities this brings. Even if, in the back of our minds, we know that we need to look at the situation and deal with it rationally as long as our emotions are running high they will dominate.

Similarly, with the buff coloured envelope arriving on the door mat. Our immediate reaction may be one of anger or frustration at yet another invoice. The adult brain knows not to jump to conclusions and open the envelope but the chimp has jumped in and responded first. Until we give the adult brain the chance to respond and decide to open the envelope we will continue with these feelings.

What happens next depends on our ability to control the chimp, to control our emotions. If we do not control the chimp, then the emotions may rage out of all proportion with the event, or worse still we may be stuck in an emotional state, far longer than is helpful or healthy. In the extreme, this may lead to fixed ways of (chimp) thinking, denying our adult brain the opportunity to deal with the change on a balanced and rational basis. To use the example above, if we fear opening the envelope and delay, then the fear perpetuates and grows. Eventually, it grows out of proportion with the likelihood of the envelope containing an invoice so we delay even further. Eventually, when our adult brain takes over and we open the envelope, there may be a sense of relief that it is not as bad as the fear had become. In extreme cases some people will never open the envelope and put it to one side – the chimp is now in total control.

Alternatively, if and when we are able to control the emotion then we give our adult brain the opportunity to review the situation and make an informed decision. When processing change of any scale we must recognise two critical factors:

1. At any given point in the journey are our emotions overwhelming our adult brain, or are they in check and the adult brain is able to deal with the change?

2. Rational decisions and control of the change is only possible by the adult brain.

Feelings and emotions are a natural part of change and the process of dealing with change. Therefore, moving through the change curve requires acknowledging the emotions that go with it, controlling the emotions to allow the adult brain to process the change, and making sure it is the adult brain that takes actions and decisions, and not the chimp.

How do we do this? Let's start by looking at how we do not do it. We cannot deny our emotions. We cannot use sheer will-power to contain them. It is like telling someone to 'cheer up', or 'don't be sad'. It cannot be done and will often just increase the emotions or spark new ones.

Venting

Our emotions have to be expressed and vented before they can be controlled. Critically, this has to be done in a 'safe' environment. Individuals releasing their emotions in a completely unchecked way are usually considered to be 'out of control'. This is not necessarily negative but has to be done in an environment that is supportive. In the context of responding to change, this means an environment where expressing those emotions can be done without adversely impacting the change or the individuals involved. For example, someone going through an organisational change at work should probably not express their full frustration or anger with their line manager. This would be better vented with a friend first and then expressed to the manager in a more controlled and balanced manner, i.e. an adult-adult conversation.

Remember that people will move backwards and forwards through the change curve and will feel different emotions at different times. With large scale change, such as trauma or bereavement, this can feel like waves of emotion. The individual will appear to alternate between adult rational thinking and behaviour and being overcome with emotion. Similarly, the venting of emotions is not necessarily a sole occurrence when dealing with change. Something that is small in scale may have a brief period of frustration or anger, but something on a larger scale may have periods of frustration, sadness, and despondency.

The purpose of expressing our emotions in this context is to acknowledge them and listen to our chimp. By doing so, we give voice to the emotions and reach a point where the emotions can be considered heard and acknowledged. Our adult brain, then, has an opportunity to engage. Venting is not to allow our emotions go unchecked and without limit. It is not a license to go over the top. When the emotions have been expressed satisfactorily, no more, no less, that is the point to listen to the adult brain.

Inner Dialogue

As soon as, the adult brain is able to engage with the change there is an inner dialogue with the chimp. We have all experienced these inner struggles where the rational adult brain is in debate with our emotions. While the emotions subside, the adult brain is able to engage with the change and take a rational view of its implications.

As an example, consider the scenario of a missed flight and arriving at an airport with your family a few minutes after the check-in has closed for your departure (yes, I have experienced that as well). The immediate emotional response will dominate all thinking. The frustration, disappointment, perhaps anger at the cause of delay, will probably be aimed at the check-in clerk. An emotional response from the family members will only further the emotional thinking and feelings that go with it. Eventually, when this has been satisfactorily expressed, the adult brain with its rational thoughts will intervene. At this point, we may have passed the dip of depression in the change curve and our adult brain will put forward suggestions as we enter the experiment stage of the curve. The adult brain will look at options for rescheduling the flight, or using other airlines, or other modes of transport to reach the destination. Each of these will have their own emotional response and reaction. There will be an inner dialogue between the adult and emotional parts of the brain while the options are considered. Sometimes, the emotions will still be too strong and decisions will be taken despite knowing they are not the best options. For example, to enter an argument with the airline staff because it feels good (expressing the emotions) and in the vain hope that they will let you through. The adult brain will know that this is not going to happen. The best option will be, as a result of the adult brain, taking over and making a decision not to listen to the emotions anymore and to take the rational decision of booking another flight.

The key point to note about this dialogue is that it is just that – a dialogue. The chimp, our emotions, should not dictate or command the adult how to respond. The adult brain has a choice. In these situations, we can decide whether to listen to our emotions and pander to them (give them more time to vent), or whether to follow our adult brain and rational thinking.

Caring for Your Chimp

Just because our adult brain has taken over does not mean we can ignore our emotions. We have all felt times when our emotions are bubbling under the surface and it can feel like we are struggling to keep them in check. In the weeks, months, and even years following the events of 7/7, and losing my wife, there were many moments when the emotions would resurface. Although this was to be expected, and is for anyone going through significant change, there are ways of caring for your chimp to avoid these becoming painful or taking up too much of your energy.

Recognition and Reward

In the days and weeks that followed 7/7 every journey on the London Underground was stressful. If the train stopped in the tunnel between stations, I could physically feel my stress level increase. But once I had completed the journey I could pat myself on the back and congratulate myself for doing it. Recognising the achievement was an important part of recognising the needs of my emotions. Every morning on my way to work, when the train reached Edgware Road station, the urge to get off and walk the rest of the way was huge. But I was not prepared to let this become a habit or superstition. I stayed on the train as it passed the site of the explosion. Once I had done this several times I rewarded myself with the indulgence of getting off to walk – almost as a treat because I knew that was what it was.

We can all do this when faced with high emotions or the risk of emotions erupting. Recognise they exist and they are valid. Recognise when you have not let them get the better of a situation and reward yourself.

Distraction

We have all encountered this. The times when something is weighing heavily on our minds but we are occupied with something that has to be done. The temporary distraction is a relief. Or we have woken in the middle of the night with our minds mulling over the same problems until we distract ourselves with a book, or something else to break the cycle. Following my wife's death, when the grief was all consuming, I had to maintain an almost constant state of distraction. Not to be occupied meant allowing my mind to wallow in the loss and emotions. We cannot maintain this – to do so would be to deny the emotions and run the risk of deferred grief. But for the times when we need or want to keep our emotions under control, distraction is a very effective technique.

For the times, when we need to keep our chimp under control, and allow our adult brain to take charge, distraction is a great technique. However, when we are doing this, consciously we should also recognise that there will be times when we need to allow our chimp time to play (to vent). There will be times when it is safe to do so, and we do not need our adult brain to be in charge, so we can turn to our emotions and let the chimp free. As much as I used distraction to help me cope with my grief, I also allowed myself time to express the emotions that were under the surface. Distraction cannot be a constant state.

Hot Buttons

We are all unique and so too are the needs of our chimps and the 'hot buttons' that will send them into overdrive. These hot buttons represent primal needs of our chimps. They are different for all us, and we are sensitive to different levels. Needs such as power, control, security, territory, family, ego, etc. A mother's reaction will be extreme if her child is under any sort of threat, no matter how mild. We have all come across business and political leaders that are driven by power or ego and any threat is met with extreme reaction. For an example look at any dictator, past or present, and their response to any form of criticism. If we are able to understand the needs of our chimp then we are able to find ways of satisfying those needs.

Chapter Five
Think Straight

"We become what we think about."
Earl Nightingale

Curbing your emotions and allowing your adult rational brain the chance to deal with the challenges the change brings is not enough. How we think and what we think will determine how we interpret and respond to the situation. If our thinking is negative or unhelpful we will spend time and effort on the wrong aspects of the change. If it is positive and constructive it will lead us to other actions and decisions that will have far better consequences.

Unhelpful Thinking

Unhelpful thinking styles are well documented and there are many different summaries available. Below are the types of unhelpful thinking that I have been guilty of in the past and most often see in other people:

Black and White

With this thinking something is either all doom and gloom or everything will be completely fine with no shades of grey, and no room for negotiation or compromise. In practice, of course, things are rarely like this. When facing change, particularly in the early stages, a lot of information is not known, a lot of options and possibilities have yet to be identified, and we cannot see the other possibilities. This does not mean, though, that we should not accept that they will probably arise. If we can recognise that we are taking an extreme view, either positive or negative, then we can open ourselves to the possibility of other scenarios in between.

Catastrophizing

With this type of thinking things are not just black but worse than that. It is human nature to jump to the worst case scenario when facing an unwelcome change or life-changing event, but if we can recognise that this is what we are doing then we can pull back from it. If we cannot recognise it then others can, explaining our thoughts to someone else will often help introduce a level of reason and logic.

Jumping to Conclusions

In a similar way to catastrophizing, or looking at things in only black or white, we also often jump directly to a conclusion and dismiss all other possibilities. Particularly, in the early stages of change when we are seeking a quick and easy solution we become closed to the variety of possibilities that may exist and just assume the outcome will be one extreme or another. This risk of this type of thinking, particularly if we are jumping to a negative conclusion, is that it may become a self-fulfilling prophecy if we are not open to other possibilities.

Shoulds, Coulds, and Oughts

Particularly when we are in the denial phase of any change we constantly look at what we should have, could have, or ought to have done differently. We also take it a step further and tell ourselves what we must do differently in the future to avoid this situation. Depending on the situation, we may be able to draw some valuable lessons from this but to dwell on in more than that achieves nothing. Particularly, when we are in the anger and frustration phase of the change curve, when we are looking for someone to blame and pick ourselves, it is tempting to admonish ourselves with what we should have, could have, and ought to have done differently.

Over-Generalisation

This is another form of jumping to conclusion where we think that every change or event of this nature ends in the same result. For example, every diagnosis of an illness ends with the same outcome, or every company takeover results in job losses, etc. By acknowledging this is not the case, then we open ourselves to the possibility of other outcomes. Every change situation is different because we all have unique circumstances and we are all unique individuals, even if the trigger event is the same.

Mind Filter

With this form of thinking we become blinkered – we only see one aspect of ourselves or the situation. Typically, we will focus on our faults or the negative aspects of a situation and our views become unbalanced. For example, we might say 'I am always doing that…', or 'that always happens to me…' Our thinking becomes filtered so we only interpret the event in one way.

Disqualifying Positives

Sometimes, we take the mind filter a stage further and even if someone points out a positive aspect of ourselves or a change situation then we dismiss it as not applying to us.

Emotional Reasoning

With this form of negative thinking we work backwards from our emotions, usually to the wrong conclusions. E.g. I feel embarrassed, therefore, I must have made a mistake, or I feel guilty so I must have done something wrong. If our adult brain is allowed to interject, we will examine the feelings and find the true root cause or challenge the emotion.

Guilt

Guilty thinking and feeling can take over our minds. This is similar to the 'Should have – Could have – Ought to have' thinking but with added self-punishment. It can also strike when we are looking at the consequences of change, are options for dealing with it, even when looking at the opportunities the change may bring. It can be triggered when feeling positive and hopeful and can be completely irrational. Someone still grieving for a loved one will feel guilty about laughing at a joke or enjoying the sun on their face. Survivors of a serious incident, such as the London bombs, will feel guilt just by surviving, or not being as injured as badly as the next person. It is irrational to everybody else but has to be overcome by the individual.

Labelling

Assigning labels to ourselves, or worse still accepting labels that other people give us, e.g. silly, daft, slow, unreliable, etc. We take a single event in a moment of time and use it to justify a label, or to validate a label that others apply. Even though there may be many more examples that disprove the label we still accept it.

Blame and Personalisation

Whether we blame ourselves for something we did or did not do, or blame others, for something they did or did not do, blame is a personal attack. There may well be a fault to be corrected, learned from, or simply avoided in the future. However, applying blame is a short lived emotional negative response.

STOPP It!

Recognising that your thinking is negative or unhelpful is the trigger to stop it. Turning around your thinking to become positive and constructive will take time and conscious effort. Use the model below to stop negative thinking and move in to a positive thinking style

S	**Stop** • Pause your current thinking and take a mental step back from the current situation • Move to a different environment, and take a short break if it helps
T	**Take a breath** • Take three slow deep breathes • Use breathing relaxation techniques to calm and clear your mind of unhelpful thoughts
O	**Observe what is happening** • What are you thinking and feeling? • What are the things going around in your head that are not settling? • Where are my thoughts focused?
P	**Perspective** • What do you know is fact and what is fiction or opinion? • How would someone else view the situation? • How would I advise someone else going through the same thing? • Just how important is it? Will I be dealing with this in six months' time or will it be a distant memory?
P	**Practise what works** • What works for me? • What will be the most helpful action to take? And why? • Am I being true to my values and what is important to me?

Table STOPP It Model

Helpful Thinking

Dealing with the effects of the 7/7 bomb and the way my life had changed, and also then losing my wife, forced me to challenge my thinking and develop techniques that have helped me cope. Some of these required no thought and were a direct result of my experiences, and others I have had to work on and nurture over time.

These techniques have helped me overcome major life-changing events, and continue to help me deal with change on a regular basis. They are personal and work for me. There may be other techniques that others have used, and every individual should use what works for them.

Perspective

As the bomb exploded around me my thought was: 'If I survive, then I will never worry about jobs, houses, money, etc., ever again. As long as my family and I have our health that is all that matters.' I then thought about how we could enjoy all that life has to offer regardless of the size of house we had, our level of income, what car we drove. None of it mattered. We could still enjoy friends, family, share experiences, the countryside, fresh air, days at the beach, and so on. The best things in life really are free. Obviously, my situation at that exact moment in time was an extreme one, but one that placed everything into sharp perspective. In reality we do still need to work, and want a nice home to live in, etc., so these things are still important. But I do try not to lose sight of the perspective that surviving the bomb gave me. We can all find points in our life, or those close to us, that give us this anchor point. A reference point that we can use to put things into perspective.

Your 24-Hours

In the immediate days after the bomb, I was acutely aware that I might not have lived to see those days. My life could so easily have ended on 7/7. Waking up and facing each day I made a conscious decision that I would get something of value, something positive out of each day. We still have to sleep, eat, commute, work, look after the children, and do all the other things that go with our day-to-day existence. Within that though we can create and enjoy valuable moments. It might be doing a good deed for a friend or relative, it might be taking just a few minutes out to have some quality one-to-one time with your children, it could be doing something to help and support a colleague above and beyond the call of duty. It can be anything, anything where your existence and being there made a difference, no matter how small.

Every human being on the planet is given the same 24 hours in a day. On any given day, we all have the same opportunity to use that time. The day (date) never existed in time before, and will never exist again, it is here now. So how are you going to use it? I was determined not to waste a day. That does not mean packing the full 24-hours with life enriching experiences, it means going to sleep at the end of the day being able to count your blessings and the good you have done during the day.

Ditch the Baggage

The next consequence of my experience on 7/7, and particularly after losing my wife and taking on full responsibility for the children and our home, was to immediately stop worrying about what other people thought of me, the actions I was taking, and the decisions I was making. This was partly out of necessity because I did not have the emotional energy to worry about it, but mainly because I realised how futile it was. Given how short life can be, and how tenuous our grip on life is, worrying about how others perceive us is wasted energy.

But if we are not worrying about how others view us then by what standard do we measure our actions? In deciding not to worry about others I was implicitly deciding to manage my life by my own standards – so they better be good. Not worrying about the views of others does not mean we can be irresponsible. If anything, it means we have to take more accountability for our actions and set our own standards accordingly.

Emotions Are Justified

Similarly, I stopped worrying what people thought about my emotions or the mood I was in at any given time. If I was having a bad day, then so be it. If anyone had a problem with it, then it was their problem, not mine. In dealing with change, particularly major change, emotions are to be expected and I was not going to make excuses for mine. This equally applied to positive feelings and emotions. If I was having a good day while others were struggling with the same change and thought I should be too, then I was not going to let them bring me down or make me feel guilty. Everyone has control of their emotions by changing their thinking. It was a positive choice not to justify or excuse my emotions to anyone.

Integrity

This led me to really think about my core values and what is important to me. It also led me to question comments that people had made about me in the past and how much value I gave them. If I was not going to worry about others views going forward, then what about how I had taken them in the past. As a natural introvert, people had commented on this in the past both in a professional and personal setting, often with negative connotations. Only now could I see that I did not have to accept that or agree with it, and in fact that in many ways it is a strength and a value. I give this as an example of how acting with integrity means being true to oneself.

It also led me to reconsider the stereo-typical view of strengths and weaknesses. Many personal character traits are labelled as such but this is completely wrong. All aspects of our character collectively define who we are. None are better than others, none are more valuable than others. If other people interpret them as such, for example in the workplace where you are expected to conform to a role, that is flawed thinking on their part. If others label us as too loud, quiet, chaotic, controlling, friendly, not friendly enough, and so on, that is their label that they are applying.

Leaders and Followers

The comment I most regularly received after the events I have been through, and still receive now, is how strong I am and have been. As anyone with similar experience will confirm, we all have an inner strength that we can find when we have to. Many people I have spoken to since, and many people reading this book, will have faced major life-changing events and have dealt with them successfully.

We all have strengths we do not know about until we need to call on them. Often, we will have strengths that other people do not. We will cope with some situations better than others and we will respond in a way that others do not. We all have moments in our lives when our strengths come to the fore we become the 'leaders', and others that we may have looked to in the past for guidance and leadership appear only to follow.

Self-Confidence

Have you ever noticed that the people most successful in a certain field or aspect of their lives appear to be the most confident? Often people will recognise they need to be more confident, and others (unhelpfully) will say the same. Confidence is not something you can switch on and switch off. It comes with recognising where your strengths lay, recognising that the things that you and others may have labelled as weaknesses are not at all, measuring yourself by your own standards, and above all, acknowledging your successes.

The way that my thinking changed after the bomb, and losing my wife, as I have shown above led to my self-confidence increasing because I was increasingly comfortable with who I was. Particularly, after I could see the results for myself and acknowledged them to myself. Just as I did not worry about how others perceived me, I did not need their recognition of how well I was coping. Taking time to celebrate successes, no matter how small, is vital.

Serenity Prayer

The serenity prayer is one of very few quotations I have put on the wall. Whether you are religious or not the call for wisdom applies to us all:

> God grant me the serenity
> To accept the things I cannot change;
> Courage to change the things I can;
> And wisdom to know the difference.

An Open Mind

Many of the negative thinking styles reflect a closed way of thinking, whether it be jumping to conclusions, catastrophizing, black and white thinking, mind filters, etc. Having an open mind opens our 'selves' to other possibilities, other solutions, other eventualities. But more than this we have to be open to accepting that some of those solutions and outcomes may not become apparent until we are further along the change curve and have made further progress in processing the change.

This was particularly true for me following the passing of my wife in 2011. I had no idea how I was going to cope with every aspect of my life that was changing. I did not know what arrangements I could or would need for looking after the children in my absence, how I would balance work and home life, and so on. It would have been very easy to catastrophize, or jump to a conclusion. However, I had to move ahead with the confidence or faith that there would be solutions, there would be a way of dealing with all the consequences, and be open to working these out as I went along.

You Are Not the First

It is very easy when faced with a new change or challenge to become focused on it, and to have a narrow field of focus. The greater the change and stresses that go with it, the more it consumes our thoughts and the more blinkered we become. A very useful open thinking style is to remember that you are not the first person to have faced this particular change or challenge.

If you acknowledge that this is correct, then it raises a number of possibilities. What have other people done in this situation? How have they overcome it? Who do you know that has relevant experience that can help? It also implies that the challenge can be, and has been, overcome before. This in turn leads to exploring solutions and broadening our thinking beyond our own narrow focus, and assuming that the challenge is unique to us.

Control

Many of the examples above of helpful thinking reflect the fact that we have far more control over our lives than we imagine. Control implies decisions and many people identify only the major decisions in life as the control they have, what determines their future. Worse still, many believe that if they are not given the opportunities they cannot make those decisions and do not have control over the direction their life takes.

For example, getting married, accepting a job, choosing a home, emigrating, starting a family are all major decisions in life. But in addition to this we all make decisions on a day-to-day, week-to-week basis. We decide what time we are going to get up (early and exercise or lay into the last possible moment?), what we eat (healthy or junk?), how we tackle our next job at work (to the best of ability or just enough to still get paid?), how to respond to our friends and colleagues (take a minute to ask how they are or dismiss them?), and so on. All of these micro-decisions have enormous bearing on our lives, self-esteem, and relationship with others. Chaos theory dictates that even a minor action can change the rest of our lives. Perhaps the colleague wanted to share a job opportunity? Perhaps doing the job better would have led to a pay rise? Our lives are dictated by hundreds of small decisions we make every day about how we interact with others, what we do, and how we spend our time.

Control applies not just to the practical examples given above but also our thinking. By questioning why we are feeling a certain way we can identify the thinking that lead to it. By questioning and challenging those thoughts we can change them. These are also decisions we make, and also show the control we actually have.

Chapter Six
Opportunity in Change

"The only sane response to change is to find the opportunity
in it."

Jeff Jarvis

There are opportunities in all change. Even if the event itself
that triggered the change is overwhelmingly negative there
will be opportunities. Even in the middle of the change curve
when all we can see are the negative effects and what we have
lost there will be opportunities to be discovered. This does not
mean the opportunities will outweigh the grief or
disappointment of the change but they will make acceptance
of the change easier.

How can there be opportunity after a terrorist bomb? One
of the victims of 7/7 was Martine Wright. She was on the
Circle Line at Aldgate when another of the bombs exploded.
Martine lost both legs and has suffered far greater injury than
I. Since then she has represented Great Britain in Sitting
Volleyball and received an MBE for her services to sport. Of
course she would rather not be in this situation, but she has
found opportunity in adversity and taken advantage of it. For
me the opportunity came from a new found sense of valuing
every day and life to come. From taking opportunities that
perhaps I would not have done in the past, such as starting a
business. Or from doing something that I had never imagined,
such as a writing this book. Both of these things have
happened years after the events that changed my life, and both
are things that I probably would never have done.

Would I turn back the clock if I could? I put this down as another negative thinking style. What has happened has happened. The opposite positive thinking style is to recognise the positive things that have happened and the opportunities it has given me, but I can only do this now after I have dealt with the change and emerged the other side.

Timing

We can only see the opportunities for ourselves when we are ready to, generally when we are coming out of the dip of depression and starting to experiment with possibilities. There is little value in trying to look for opportunities if you are still reeling from the shock or surprise of the change, in denial, or gripped with depression and despondency about the change. Even when others are trying to support you by pointing out the possibilities these will not be heard until we are ready.

As we start to look at the possibilities the change brings, the options open to us, the decisions we need to make, there will be opportunities. Only as we move forward and start to make decisions in dealing with the change will we see the opportunities. The new direction we take will often lead to opportunities long after the event itself. Ultimately we may only recognise the opportunities when we look back.

Let me take a common example. Losing a job or redundancy is a significant life-changing event for us all and something many people have experienced. With very rare exception, we are in work out of necessity, so losing a job often has serious consequences. As described earlier in the book in the initial part of the change curve we will be in shock, often angry, worried, and in despair. We may even be in denial for a period of time and not accepting of the situation. After a while depression will set in and we will only see the negative impacts and consequences. Only when we start to look at options for moving forward we will see opportunities. We may consider new job opportunities that are perhaps better suited to us, we may consider starting a business with all the opportunities that brings, we may even consider relocating to a different part of the country or a different country all together! This is not to say that all options will be full of opportunity or even an easy route to follow, but neither will they be totally negative and difficult.

Practise!

We can use everyday changes to our lives to be open to the possibility of opportunities and actively look for them. The great benefit of this is that it makes us more open to accepting change and turning a change to our advantage as much as possible.

The next time there is a change to your day, practise looking at the opportunities as well as the negative effects. A cancelled meeting may disrupt your diary and mean a decision is delayed, but it also means you have some free time in your day and have more time to prepare for the meeting. A cancelled dinner with friends is disappointing, but it also means you have time to do those little jobs you want to do and still reschedule the dinner for a more convenient time. Looking for and spotting the opportunities is a great way of managing the emotional reaction and accepting change.

As with any change in behaviour, the more it is practised the more it becomes ingrained in our habits and routines. By constantly looking for the opportunities that arise with change it will eventually become instinct. If we can learn to do this then we will automatically see change as also an opportunity, possibly even welcomed.

Good Company

There are many people that have faced major life-changing events, or even been born with serious disabilities, but would not change their lives:

Malala Yousafzai

Yousafzai was born in Mingora, Swat, Pakistan. Inspired by her father and mother who ran a local school, in 2009 when she was just 11, Malala wrote a blog for BBC Urdu, under a pseudonym, about life under Taliban occupation. She then worked with the New York Times to make a documentary as the Pakistani Military were intervening in the region. Her life changed in 9th October 2012 when she was shot by a Taliban gunman on her way to school.

When she was stable enough she was transferred to the Queen Elizabeth hospital in Birmingham. In the weeks and months that followed there was a national and international outpouring of support for Malala. She has since made a full recovery. Rather than be defeated and silenced by the attack Malala has become a prominent education activist. She continues to speak out against the suppression of children, and supports the right of education for all. She has won numerous awards and prizes, and was a co-recipient of the 2014 Noble peace prize. She, now, has a voice, and opportunities to speak out, that perhaps she would never have had.

Stephen Hawking

The late Stephen Hawking had a brilliant mind and his intellect was clear for all to see during his school years. He was born into an intellectual family who placed a high value on education. He attended Radlett School in Hertfordshire, and then St Albans school, also in Hertfordshire, after passing the 11-plus a year early. At 17 he began his University education studying Physics and Chemistry at University College, Oxford.

He was diagnosed with Motor Neurone disease when he was just 21-years-old and given a prognosis of two years to live. He sunk into depression and although encouraged to carry on with his work, he could see no point with the end of his life supposedly so near. The rest of his story is highly publicised and Stephen Hawking became the most famous physicist of our time. Not only did Stephen Hawking work through the change curve but he went on to take every possible professional and personal opportunity that came his way, to live a fulfilled life to the best of his ability.

Piper Kerman

Piper had a comfortable life living in a New York City apartment, with a promising career, and a caring boyfriend. Her life changed when two customs officials arrived at her door and she was charged with drug trafficking offences. Ten years earlier Piper had been romantically involved with a member of a drug gang and had carried the proceeds of a deal across the border. Her past caught up with her and she was sentenced to 15 months in prison.

The experience could have crushed her and destroyed her life, but she did not let it. She went on to publish the memoirs of her time in prison, 'Orange is the new Black: My Year in a Women's Prison' that became an international best seller and was adapted for television. Kerman continues to speak out about the American justice system, the federal prison system, and women's experience in prison. Kerman serves on the board of the Women's Prison Association and is regularly invited to speak about her experiences and views.

Frank Gardner

Following a career as an investment banker Frank Gardner followed his dream and took up a career in journalism. In 1998 he became the BBC's first full-time correspondent in the Gulf and after the September 11 attacks in 2011 Frank specialised in covering stories on the 'War on Terror'. He was well suited to the role having read Arabic and Islamic Studies at Exeter University.

Everything changed for Frank on June 6, 2004 while reporting from the Al-Suwaidi district of Riyadh, Saudi Arabia. He was shot six times and his attackers only left because they believed he was dead. In the attack his cameraman, Simon Cumbers, was killed. Frank was very close to death. His surgeon later told him that he would have died within two hours of being rescued. He had the extreme good fortune to be treated by a South African surgeon with extensive experience of gunshot wounds. Without being rescued just in time, and having the right surgeon, Frank would not have survived.

Despite the trauma of these events Frank Gardner returned to his job at the BBC. Not only does he continue as a BBC security correspondent but he also reports on location as well as from the studio. He as very successfully worked through the emotional roller coaster of the change curve and been able to separate his emotions from rational thinking. He has made the right decisions for him, for the right reasons.

The examples above are all high profile individuals that have been through brutal and traumatic changes in their lives. They have had to go through the challenges and emotions of the change curve, but have emerged at the other end and taken advantage of the opportunities that have arisen. There are opportunities within all change, and as a result of all change. This applies to all of us, not just high profile figures, and not just as a result of major life changing events. There are new opportunities that will follow the breakdown of a relationship, the loss of a job, a cancelled meeting, a car breakdown, and so on. Looking for the opportunities is a positive thinking style that makes it easier to decide on options, and come to acceptance of the change.

Chapter Seven
The New Normal

"The secret of change is to focus all of your energy not on fighting the old, but on building the new."

Socrates

As we move through the change curve, possibly moving backwards and forwards, at times we will look beyond the dip of depression and consider the future. If we are able to do this with our adult brain and not through the fog of emotion, then we can consider the possibilities the change may bring and the options and decisions we will face. We will probably fall back into depression at times and it may well take several periods of forward thinking before we feel comfortable to move on and take positive steps.

Options

Most types of change, particularly major life-changing events, will lead to a number of possible actions that can be taken or possible scenarios for the future. Some of these will be obvious and clear to us – and others we may not see at all, or at least not until we go exploring and investigate the possibilities. Again, this applies to all types of change of whatever scale.

To take a major life-changing example, such as the loss of a loved one, this can have all sorts of practical implications such as financial issues, managing the home, maintaining the home, raising children, supporting other family members, and so on. In each case there will be options and possible solutions. Some of these will be more palatable than others and considering the options, and the implications, may well provoke an emotional reaction pushing us back into the dip of depression.

A more trivial example, such as a car breakdown, has a variety of implications. How to get the car fixed, how to pay for it, how to manage without it while it is being repaired, etc. Similarly, in each case there are options and possible solutions, which also may invoke an emotional response.

Only by exploring these options and solutions will we get to understand them and identify other possibilities. This is the experimental stage of the change curve and it is how we start to navigate our way through implementing and accepting the change.

Not an Option

Some people will not face up to the decisions that need to be made and will drift into the default 'do nothing' option. Either because they are not able to face the challenge of taking positive steps to determine their way forward, or because none of the possible scenarios seem acceptable. Doing nothing is the least favourable option because progress will only be made when there is no other choice. At this point there may not be any other options apart from the one that is forcing the issue.

To use the car breakdown example above, the consequence of doing nothing is that the car will sit on the drive or in the road and not get repaired. It will deteriorate further and become even more difficult and expensive to repair. In the mean time we become used to using public transport and eventually give up on the car. In the extreme example it will sit there until we move house and we are forced to have it towed away for scrap. You have probably seen cars like this. There may have been a good reason for not getting the car repaired promptly, such as the cost. However, looking at options such as getting a quote, or selling it at the time, would have been better options that doing nothing.

Doing nothing, and waiting until we are forced to take action, really is not an option. However, this is different to taking your time to understand your options and becoming comfortable enough to start making decisions. Sometimes procrastination is due not to shying away from a decision but because we do not yet feel comfortable to make the decision. In this case we need to ask why? It may be, and will very probably be, due to not having all the information we need. If we do not understand all the implications of a possible decision, then we may not be comfortable with the risk.

After the events of 7/7, and then losing my wife, there were enormous questions to be answered, and ultimately decisions to be taken. Should I stay at home for my children or continue to go to work? How was I to cope with all the housework, laundry, shopping etc.? How was I to cope with the physical and emotional child care that my wife was so good at? How was I even to make sure the children got to school and had someone to come home to every day? Then there were things like supporting them with their homework or even the practicalities of getting to clubs and after-school activities. On the face of it there were no answers, but by looking at the options and experimenting with different solutions (and with a great deal of help) I found a way through. Doing nothing and not facing up to these challenges was not an option. It would have led to chaos, an untidy home, poorly cared for children, and nothing would have happened without intervention.

Taking Control

When we understand our options and the decisions we need to take, we are in a position to take control. This is the turning point in progressing through the change curve. By taking action and making decisions we feel empowered and more in control. We become less a victim of the change and more a master of it. Each decision we take and each action we take brings as step closer to the end of the change curve and acceptance and integration of the change.

As we take decisions, and take action, we start process the change in practical terms and move towards acceptance. Each step may give rise to new issues or new decisions that need to be taken, but it may also give rise to new opportunities that we previously could not see. Only by taking the first steps in dealing with change are we able, not only to move forward, but uncover other possibilities to help us accept the change.

Integration

As we come out of the change curve having investigated our possibilities and taken action on some of them, we are at a point of accepting the change and moving forward. Making the decisions we need to deal with the change, and taking actions to apply them, we have accepted the change and integrated it into our lives. What was a big disruption has now been accommodated and our lives once again take on a level of normality. This will be different to our original plans and expectations; it will be a new normal. Even if it was only a small scale change, as we come out of the change curve we have dealt with the change and accepted it.

The new normal is characterised by stability, routine, and lack of emotional extremes. We now have a new frame of reference, a new set of expectations that are now being fulfilled as we are taking a new direction aligned with those expectations. We have adapted to the change.

In many cases the change, or trigger event, will have impacted people other than ourselves, often those closest to us. It may have also impacted family, friends, or work colleagues. All of whom will be processing the change at different speeds. Just because we have accepted the change and are ready to move forward does not mean that everybody else will have. It may be that some have reached this point before us and do not understand why we have not. It may also be that we have reached it before others and assume others are at the same point. This difference can give rise to tension between the individuals involved that pulls people back into the change curve.

New Change

As our lives move to adopt a 'new normal' way of being, we are accepting that our expectations and plans have changed. We now have a new vision of our future.

At the same time the emotional responses to the change will have subsided. We may still have periods of emotion in relation to the change but they will be fewer and further between. This means the change is consuming less emotional energy than it did in the early days.

With these two factors combined, more emotional energy to spare, and a new view of what our future looks like, we are now open or susceptible to new change. We have a new view of what normal looks like but change is constant. Something will come along to challenge our view of the new normal again and we will embark on a new change curve. The more stable and settled we are with our 'new normal' the more open we become to being influenced and impacted by even smaller changes.

Following the London bombs of 7/7 it took years for me to fully accept what had happened. Initially my profound sense of value and gratitude at still being here to enjoy each day, and new found perspective, meant that I could brush off the more mundane changes that came along. A change of plans for the day was not a problem, a broken appliance at home was trivial, an unexpected bill of no consequence.

Compared to the possibility of losing my life and not being here these things irrelevant. However, as time progressed, my heightened awareness of the value of each day subsided, and day to day routines took over. I was still very aware of my new perspective, and the experience of 7/7 etched in my mind, but it did not dominate my thoughts any more. After time I started to realise that small changes were impacting me more than they had done previously, and my reactions were more normal and in-line with others. I had progressed sufficiently through the change, and my life stabilised again, such that I was susceptible to the more routine changes we all face. I took it as a positive sign of progress, but still try to keep my sense of perspective alive.

Chapter Eight
External Influences

"You are the average of the five people you spend most time with."

Jim Rohn

Managing our emotions and engaging our adult brain in positive and constructive thinking is largely about using our mind. It is about internal influence, whether that be controlling negative emotions, fostering positive emotions, applying rational thinking, and taking steps to move our lives forward. All of this is largely an internal process.

It is equally important to consider the external influences that shape our lives. This is mainly other people, the relationships we have, family members, close friends, colleagues, but even casual acquaintances can all have an impact. There are other external factors that can impact us. Time is another major factor – if we are under time pressure, or have deadlines imposed on us, or even just short of time to deal with the emotions, and take thinking time. There can also be other elements of our lives that add to our pressures and stress, for example practicalities like commuting, or childcare, or home maintenance, and so on. Anything that adds additional pressure or stress will often impact our emotional reasoning in other areas. By identifying these factors we can sometimes remove them or at least limit their influence.

People

The biggest external influence on our lives is the people around us. This is everyone we interact with whether it be family, friends, colleagues, customers, team mates, etc. All of these people will have an influence on us – sometimes very minor and sometimes it will be very significant. It does not matter if it is someone we spend a lot of time with or just a passing acquaintance. Sometimes the people we hardly see are the most observant and say the most profound things.

Family members and close friends will often feel at liberty to say whatever they think and give you their opinion whether it is welcome or not. They may even feel they have a right to have a say, e.g. if there are consequences for them or other family and friends. This may or may not be justified but their input and 'advice' should be taken as just that. It does not have to be followed – that is a decision for you to take, or not, depending on what you think of it and your respect for the judgement of the person providing it.

Other people, such as colleagues, friends, and even people you may have only just met, will often pass comment if the subject comes up. Sometimes this can be helpful and insightful, but other times it can ignorant and naïve (someone having no understanding or empathy).

The real test is whether or not they are supportive, constructive, give you energy and motivation, or spark negativity and bring you down? How do you feel after spending time with them? Have they left you feeling positive and hopeful or unhappy or worried? You are largely in control of the people you surround yourself with and spend time with. Even if there are people you have to interact with, such as work colleagues, or a customer, for example, if they are not positive and supporting you can limit your interaction and contain the discussion to what suits you.

As difficult as it may be, removing negative influences from our lives, or at least minimising their chance to have this influence, is critical. Surrounding yourself with those who are supporting and encouraging will make a significant difference. In the face of change and challenge, it will become very clear who are the supporters, who are the detractors, and those who really do not care either way. Use this information and surround yourself with people that care. These should be people you are prepared to listen to. They have input you want to hear, and have advice you are willing to consider.

To take this a stage further, you can 'stand on the shoulders of giants', i.e. look around you for the people who cannot just provide the support you need, but who will actively help you move forwards, and deal with whatever challenges you are facing. This is not a sign of weakness in needing help, but a sign of strength and confidence in recognising the experience of others and how it can benefit you.

Time

Time can influence our lives in many ways, particularly when we are trying to deal with change and the emotional and practical drain that goes with it. When we feel that we do not have enough time to do what is needed then we feel additional stress. Similarly, if our time is taken up with activities that we see no value or point in they become disheartening and we become demotivated. In both cases this is a negative influence on our lives which takes energy from us instead of giving us energy to carry on.

For me this was particularly true after the 7/7 London bombs. Every day, every minute, was valuable. If I had too much to do then something had to give and I would be ruthless in cutting things out of my day that were not of value.

Making time for ourselves can sometimes be difficult but it is not impossible. Start by prioritising and identifying the one or two things that absolutely have to be done that day. There may be none that fall into this category so pick the one or two highest priority tasks and deal with those. Review your plans for the day and remove anything that does not have to be there. You may well identify things that can be eliminated completely. With what is left ask, 'why am I doing these things?' Are there tasks you can give to someone else, or someone else ought to be doing in the first place? Are you doing things to be helpful for others when now is the time to be helpful to yourself? Are there ways of being more productive, e.g. making (hands-free) phone calls from the car or while out walking?

Time is also essential to us to deal with the emotions of change, or just to think. As well as the conscious thinking we do when an issue is front of mind, we also need to recognise the value of our sub-conscious thinking. Having some time to ourselves every day, no matter how short, gives us time to process. Many people will meditate, or exercise, or just find a quiet corner to take a break from a busy day. These are often our most productive times when dealing with thoughts and emotions and the value of this time should not be underestimated.

There are other times when having too much time, and too little to occupy ourselves, can be detrimental. Particularly when dealing with the emotional aspects of change, having too much time can sometimes allow us to wallow in emotions for longer than is good for us. In the depths of depression or grief this can feel incredibly lonely and feel like we are just sinking lower. Having time to express these emotions with others, or allowing ourselves to feel them in isolation if we require, is essential. But we should also guard against allowing these emotions to take over just because we have time and our hearts and minds are not occupied with other things.

Time is arguably our most precious resource. We have 24 hours in a day and need to make the best use of it. If we appreciate each day, then we will use it wisely. This is a very personal perspective and how we decide to use our day is unique to each of us. Removing the pressures and stress of not having sufficient time is something that each of us can address, but how we do it is unique to us, and is based on our priorities and values. However, each day is ours, and we are in control of how we use it.

Stuff and Clutter

'Things' can have the same effect as people and time. Just as children have favourite possessions that give them comfort, as adults we have spaces, places, belongings of sentimental value that we enjoy. We can indulge in these things for the same comfort when we need them. For some it might be wallowing in the bath with a good book, or it might be losing yourself in a film that you have seen many times before. It does not matter (as long as it not taken to excess). If it is of comfort when you need it then recognise it and use it. It has to be a positive influence in your life and not be allowed to become a negative one, e.g. drinking too much, eating too much, etc.

The same affect can be made by practical changes to our routine. If you can improve your day by changing your schedule, making more time for yourself, creating a new routine, then do it. All of these things fall into the category of helping yourself, and looking after yourself. It is not selfish if it is needed.

On the flip side, there can be things in our lives that are an irritation or annoyance. In which case they are a negative influence that can compound negative thoughts and feelings. They may be a drain on our time or money. They may just be something we do not like. For example, if the clutter on a shelf has always annoyed you then remove it. If meetings starting late annoy you then give them five minutes to start or walk out. If a crowded train is stressful, wait for the next one. If that broken gate is always keeping you awake at night, fix it. Again, anything that feels like a negative impact on our lives, no matter how small, can add to an emotional situation such as major change. By removing them we take the pressure off and also get a sense of satisfaction.

With all external influences, particularly in time of significant change, it is important to identify what is a positive or supportive influence, and what is not. We can take steps to use the positive influences as we need them, and to minimise or remove the negative ones. This is something that only we can judge as individuals. Others may have a view of what is positive or negative for us, what is supportive or not, and may well express their opinions without invitation. However, this is a personal judgement. Be open to the advice of others, but be wary of well-meaning advice that conflicts with your personal views and instincts.

Chapter Nine
What If?

"A clever person solves a problem, a wise person avoids it."
Albert Einstein

One of the unhelpful thinking styles that we all adopt, even if briefly, is to consider what we 'should have', 'could have', or 'ought to have' done to avoid a situation or unwelcome change. Some events, such as the London bombings, are totally unexpected and no one could have predicted the horrible events of that day. In hindsight we may consider 'if only…' but there is nothing any of those involved that day could reasonably be expected to have done to avoid the situation.

Many other situations are more likely to be encountered as we go through our lives, and some we may even be able to predict. For example, a family history of a medical condition increases our chances of inheriting it and is something we could possibly takes steps to avoid or at least be prepared for. Similarly, the writing is often on the wall before organisations make major changes or go out of business. Taking up a dangerous sport carries risks and injuries can be expected. Often with a little forethought we can anticipate the change events that will seriously impact our lives and plans, and even if we accept the risks, we can take steps to avoid them happening or be left in a difficult situation.

Instead of looking back and considering what we 'should have' or 'could have' done, it is far better to look forward and consider 'what if?' That is not to say we must be fearful of everything that could possibly go wrong and be paralysed as a result. Those that avoid all risks will do nothing and their life will be severely constrained and lose out. At the other extreme those that give no consideration to what may go wrong may enjoy the absolute freedom that goes with it, but will also suffer the consequences of not being prepared, and all the stresses that go with it.

One of the most shocking aspects of my experience in the 7/7 bombs, and losing my wife at such a young age, was the realisation of how fragile and tenuous life can be. Similar experiences of losing a good friend to cancer in his early 30s, as well as a business acquaintance from a simple fall on concrete stairs and the subsequent head injury, was a stark reminder that things can be taken away from us very easily. Anyone who has suddenly lost a job will know that a secure comfortable lifestyle can suddenly be jeopardised and their family and home put at risk.

Following 7/7 I made a conscious decision to make the most out of the rest of my life. Every day was a bonus that I may not have been here to see. I am sure everyone who survived that day, and similar atrocities since, will have said the same thing. But this is a very personal view and living life to the full will mean different things to different people. Some people will have quit their job, sold all their belongings, and gone off to travel the world. Some will have changed career and started a business. For others it will have simply meant spending more time with the family and friends and enjoying the things that matter.

Security in its widest sense, i.e. to know that our future is secure, our income, our family, our dreams, is one of the most primitive human needs. Whatever that future looks like, we want to keep it secure so it makes sense to consider what might threaten it. This is a very personal view and will mean different things to different people. For someone who lives for sport the risks may come from possible injury – either playing or from other activities. For someone who lives for the ability to play music the risks may be to their hands, or ears. Others may be motivated by travel in which case the risks might be anything that impacts their freedom to travel. Whatever the vision of our future that we want to protect, spending a little time considering the threats to that future and what can be done to avoid them is time well spent.

Balance

Drawing the right balance between taking a risk or not, and the implications for how this dictates what we do or do not, is a personal choice. Very few people have no one to consider. Young, single people may be carefree but they will have parents, siblings, close friends, all of whom would be impacted should anything happen to them. Those with husbands, wives and children will be acutely aware of the responsibility they have. If nothing else, we have our own dreams for the future and we want to live them as much as possible.

We should all consider 'what if' and then decide on the action we want to take. It may be to accept the risks because of the thrill of what we are about to embark on is worth it. Or we may decide that actually the risks are too great to justify, or that we should take steps to reduce the risk.

Look to the Future

Before you can spend any time asking 'what if' and potentially avoid some of the pitfalls ahead, you have start with your views of what the future looks like and what is of value.

For the person that has always wanted to travel the world, quitting a job and going for it will not be considered a risk but an absolute necessity! For others who value securing their family's future, quitting a job would be a foolish thing to do.

Only by having a vision of your future life and being clear in your own heart and mind on what is of value can you possible consider how best to protect it.

Ask The Question – What if?

When you are clear on your vision of the future and what you value then you can ask the question 'what if':

- What could go wrong? Or right?
- What is the most probable outcome?
- What has happened to other people in this situation?
- What was the impact?
- How would I cope?

For example, those whose priority is protecting their family will consider what would happen if they lost a job? Or had a serious injury or illness? Those that live for their sport will take steps to avoid common injuries. Some will be driven to build their business – they will consider all the risks that could lead to failure.

Other people are a great source for identifying risks – some will love to point out the possible pitfalls, just as others will be overly optimistic. When embarking on a major change it can be valuable to consider the input and experience of others, at least to satisfy yourself that you are aware of risks and have taken care to address them – to the extent you feel necessary.

Really?

Now it is time for a reality check. When considering all the things that can go wrong and the risks we need to form a realistic view, in each case we need to consider the likelihood of the problem arising. Is it something that is very likely and we need to seriously consider? Or is it just a remote possibility that we may be prepared to accept?

At the same time we need to consider the consequences of the problem arising. It may something that is likely to occur but if the implications are minimal it does not really matter. Alternatively, even if it is a remote possibility, something with severe or catastrophic impact needs to be taken seriously.

By taking this reality check on our 'what if' problems and our worries we can focus on the ones that need our attention. We should consider the risks that are likely to arise, and also the ones that are less likely but would be devastating to our hopes and plans for the future.

What Can I Do?

At this point we can look at our options. There will probably be steps we can take to reduce the risk of the worst happening. It may be taking more care of our health, keeping our skills and employability up to date, diversifying our business interests, and so on. There is usually not one but multiple things we can do to avoid unwelcome and life-changing events.

Even so, we cannot remove risk completely. Having excellent skills is not a guarantee of long-term employment – businesses go bust. Having a healthy diet and fitness regime is no guarantee against illness or injury. As well as considering what we can do to avoid a situation arising, we also need to consider what we would do if it did. We take out insurance to deal with the financial implications, or do not (and self-insure). What about other aspects of our lives? What would happen in the event or illness or injury? What would happen if a business failed? And so on.

Now What?

Having taken stock of our position, and our hopes and dreams for the future, we may feel that comfortable that we have considered the risks and taken the right steps. But as we have seen in this book, change is constant and our situation is constantly changing. Considering our future and how best to secure our hopes and dreams is not a one-time activity. We need to consider it on a regular basis and make changes accordingly. People will often do this after marriage, or starting a family. Or if they are jolted into it by seeing how others struggle following a life-changing event.

Chapter Ten
Supporting Others

"No one is useless in this world who lightens the burdens of another."

Charles Dickens.

The very first thing to consider when supporting others dealing with change is to ask 'why'? Not why should you support someone, but why are you motivated to? Is it just because you are expected to or it seems the right thing to do? Or because you genuinely have the person's best interests at heart and want to help them move forwards? Similarly, how far you are prepared to go help someone?

If you are offering support, or on the receiving end of such an offer, there are three different scenarios to consider. The empty promise, the conflict of interest, and the sincere offer.

The empty promise arises from the many people who will say 'just let me know if there is anything I can do to help' but you and they know they will not when it comes to it. Often it is the polite and expected thing to say. There is nothing wrong with being polite and offering the empty promise – as long as both parties perceive it the same way. If the recipient perceives it as a sincere offer, and attempts to take it up, they will inevitably be disappointed. Worse, this may compound their challenges further.

The conflict of interest is usually a sub-conscious conflict, but not always. Consider the organisational change and impact to a member of staff. The support offered by the manager to the sub-ordinate should have a common objective. However, in many cases the agenda and interests of the manager will not be completely aligned with that of the sub-ordinate. A more astute manager will be aware of this and conscious of the difference. Unfortunately, many do not have the training or experience to deal with it with this level of understanding.

Often the conflict of interest will be in the sub-conscious. For example, a friend may offer support to someone going through a divorce, but if that friend has their own relationship issues their sub-conscious motivation may be in sharing their own pain not necessarily getting the best result for the friend. They may feel better themselves by comparing their situation with their friend's. This is a conflict. By way of another example, consider a family member offering support to someone taking a new job in a different part of the country. Apart from missing their relative, there may be practical implications for childcare, or supporting parents, that give rise to a conflict of interest.

A conflict of interest does not undermine or negate the value in providing support – so long as it is recognised by at least one, and preferably both, parties. In this case the support offered is viewed in the correct context and judged correctly. If the person offering support recognises where the conflicts of interest arise and manages them with complete integrity, then the support is genuine and sincere.

A sincere offer of support will help an individual cope with the change and move along the change curve. It will understand and accommodate their emotions and be given without qualification or constraint. It will also involve more than just words. It will involve giving of time, practical help, emotional support, perhaps even financial support.

When supporting someone going through change we often do not have direct experience of the event or change they are going through. This can make it very difficult to relate to and therefore affect how we support them. People will often respond with 'I don't know what to say' because they do not. However, even in this case with an understanding of the change process we are better able to gauge where someone is in this and how to respond. Similarly, we can identify if their inner chimp, their emotions, are currently out of control and we are talking to the chimp rather than the adult. This allows us to communicate more effectively.

Shared Experiences

It may be that we have experienced something similar and can connect with the individual in a way that others cannot. If we have had a similar experience we recognise the feelings, the thoughts, and even the practical difficulties. In this case we can connect with the individual and share experiences. We understand the things they say and do in a way that others do not. This can apply to everything from the tragedy of grieving for a loved one, the trauma of being made redundant, or grappling with a similar experience such as leaving home. It also applies to change on a much smaller scale. Anything where we are able to link the change someone is going through to an event in our own past allows us to make comparisons and connections.

Following the bomb on 7/7 I retold my story many times over. I never had a problem relaying my experiences to those who were interested. I did this so many times I could forewarn people how long it was going to take! However, being able to talk about it in itself was little help to me other than being able to vent my thoughts and feelings. There was very little that the person I was telling the story to was able to say about it. They could not relate to the event. I could talk about what happened in great detail but I got very little in response by way of support or help. There was always a feeling that the discussion was empty or an anti-climax. All of this changed a few years later when I met someone who had also been caught up a terrorist bomb. Even though it was in a different city and a different environment (not on a train) there were huge parallels. For the first time I was able to tell my story to someone who could relate to every step, every thought, and every feeling. Although in this case he was well qualified to provide support (a member of the clergy), finally speaking to someone who understood me made a remarkable difference. From that point on I was able to move forwards through the change curve.

The more similar the experience the more we are able to relate to the individual. We can provide real empathy rather than vague sympathy. Conversely, if the experience only has tenuous similarity, attempting to provide support and comment on this basis can backfire and be ill-judged. On more than one occasion a friend or colleague would empathise and say they knew what I was talking about because they had experienced other (but completely different) life-changing events, such as a serious accident or injury within their family. This was not only of no help but made me feel their response and support had no credibility or worth. The situation was a totally different event though some of the emotions may have been similar. Judging how you respond and support someone needs to be made with great care, not just well meaning.

On the Curve

How do you judge where someone is on the change curve? Remember that people move backwards and forwards and do not move through it smoothly. Where a person was the last time you met may bear no relation to where they are this time. The factors to take into consideration are:

- How long is it since the event happened? For example, are they still in shock/surprise that the event has just happened? Has time passed and they are in dip of depression?

87

- What do their emotions to tell you? Do their emotions suggest they are at the frustration or anger stage? Or perhaps depressed? Or possibly they are feeling hopeful and positive and coming out of the curve?
- What physical environment are they in and what are they doing? Are they in an environment where they have little to do and time to dwell on the change? Are they actively in engaged in dealing with the event? Etc.
- Equally importantly, what has just happened or been said to them that influences their current state of mind? Perhaps they were positive and moving forward the last time you saw them, but a bad day or an inconsiderate word may have set them back?

Only by taking care to understand the individual and how they may currently be feeling about the change can you respond considerately.

Escaped Chimps

One of the most important aspects to consider when trying to support someone struggling with change is to understand who you are communicating with at any given time. Are you speaking to the person's adult brain and able to have a rational objective conversation? Or is it their chimp who is running wild?

For some people it will be easy to determine their emotional state because it will be very clear. Someone who is very expressive and open with their emotions will leave you in no doubt how they are feeling. If these feelings are dominating conversation, then you are probably talking to the chimp. In this case you cannot have an adult-to-adult conversation, it will be adult-to-child.

In other cases, it will be more difficult to read the emotional state of an individual. Clues will be subtle and you will need to read body language, consider the tone of voice, choice of words, etc. You will need to know the individual well to do this, but if you are genuinely wishing to provide support then you probably do.

Dealing with somebody else's inner chimp is not dissimilar to dealing with your own. Distraction is often the best solution. You do not have to pander to the chimp and respond to the emotions. By all means acknowledge them but then move the conversation on. The chimp is not in control. Moving the conversation on to practical next steps and engaging the adult brain will help contain the chimp.

Negative Thinking

If you are supporting someone who is not gripped by emotion and is able to discuss matters rationally, it may be that the individual is stuck in a cycle of negative thinking. The challenge here is to turn the thinking around and make it positive, but without undermining or arguing. Identify the negative thinking style, and there may be a number inter-mingled, and use the STOPP It! process to break the cycle.

When the opportunity arises introduce one of the positive thinking styles, and engage with the adult brain. The speed at which you can help to turn someone's thinking around from negative to positive will be dictated by them, but as long as they are willing, you can lead them gradually to change their perspective.

Chapter Eleven
Personal Change

"When we are no longer able to change a situation – we are challenged to change ourselves."

Viktor E. Frankl

Significant life-changing events, such those I experienced, will change us whether we like it or not. They will change our character, our personalities, and our behaviours. I am not the same person I was before I boarded the Circle Line train on 7/7. The events had a profound effect on me and the way that I look at the world. Sometimes we have to change ourselves in response to an external trigger event, and sometimes we are just given extra inspiration to change. For example, a health scare, of our own or someone close to us, may make us realise we have to change our diet or level of exercise.

Change Cycle

When making intentional change to our own behaviours very few people are able to make a significant change at the first attempt. For example, people that are trying to give up smoking often take several attempts, people trying to get fit will usually try a number of activities before finding the right one. With each attempt they learn more about themselves, what works, and what doesn't work.

This cycle is captured in a model by Prochaska and DiClemente (known as the Transtheoretical model) and is reflected in the diagram below.

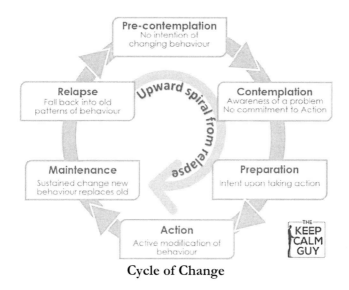

Cycle of Change

There is a process that we all go through when trying to change ourselves, and for most of us we will relapse and go through this process a number of times. It may be that we have to experiment with different approaches and different forms of support. For example, if we are trying to change a habit or start a new one, then we may try at first without support, we may then need to remove temptations that we need to avoid, we may seek alternatives, we may find someone to support us through the process, and so on. If we learn that works and what does not work then with each attempt we will have greater success.

Precontemplation

At this stage we are not ready to change. We may recognise that we should but we have any number of excuses why we cannot. We are unmotivated, unready, and unwilling to change. For example, we may know we are slightly overweight – but we do not recognise it as a problem, particularly if we have many others that are higher priority.

Contemplation

When we reach contemplation it is because the pressures or reasons to change are starting to outweigh the reasons not to. The advantages are overcoming the disadvantages. For example, we may have become more concerned about our diet, or level of fitness, or financial situation, and so on. To use the example above, if we are overweight we may have reached the point of being embarrassed of our weight or lack of fitness and the need to do something about it becomes a higher priority.

Preparation

At this stage we are ready to take action, have positive intentions, and specific actions in mind. We may have plans to join a gym, or consult a doctor, and so on. We will become more aware of the possible solutions or approach to our change and will start to formulate plans. We will make plans to join a gym, or start a regular exercise, or cut out certain foods, etc.

Action

Now we have put those actions into place and have made tangible and visible changes. We have to be careful that the actions we have taken are significant enough of have the desired effect. Visiting a gym for an application form is not the same progress as spending an hour on the equipment. Smoking 19 instead of 20 cigarettes a day helps but is not sufficient to make the change we seek. A token gesture towards change is not sufficient. We need to commit to actions that will make a difference, and preferably make the commitment to others as well as ourselves so we can be held to account.

Maintenance

This is the challenge for us all. Embedding the change into our routine, our processes, and becoming a permanent part of our lives takes time. It can take a number of years, not just weeks and months, for the change to become permanent. Maintaining the change to our behaviour is where support is critical, and using tools and techniques to avoid a relapse can make all the difference. There are always moments, particularly after a good well intentioned start, when it is tempting to relax the routine, to skip a session in the gym for example, in the mistaken belief that the change is embedded in our lives.

Relapse

A personal behavioural change will be difficult to make and very few people have the self-discipline to make it at the first attempt. This means they will relapse and ultimately go around the cycle again. You will see in the diagram this reflected in an upward spiral of learning on each iteration. Failure is success in progress and is part of the process of personal change.

Motivation

When contemplating change, we should consider our motivation. This again brings us back to the question – why? When the motivation is strong enough we will be inspired to change, we will act on it, and if the motivation remains, we will maintain the change. Conversely, if we are struggling to make change it is often because the motivation is not there or not strong enough to overcome the resistance and our excuses.

The events of 7/7 changed my perspective on life, and helped me value the things that were truly important, as well as life itself. After losing my wife, my motivation to make changes to my life was extreme. I needed to be around for my children so be able to work from home, I need to replace my salary with another form of income, and I need to create a new form security and stability in my life. Taking major steps to start my own business, give up my previous career, and make other major changes to my life were not always easy. But the motivation was strong and carried me through.

The changes I have made in my life since then are almost a total transformation. It is not just because of the experience of almost losing my life that I viewed the rest of my life as a new opportunity. Having experienced what Abraham Maslow describes as self-actualisation, i.e. complete fulfilment in all aspects of life, during the 1990s, I set about re-building my life to achieve the same level of fulfilment – and succeeded. This was not just about coping with the changes forced upon me, but learning how to embrace them, and turn them to my advantage. Rebuilding your life this way goes far beyond simply coping with change. For more information please visit my website:
www.thekeepcalmguy.co.uk

Chapter Twelve
Leading Change

"Change, like healing, takes time."
Veronica Roth

As well as dealing with change in their lives as described earlier in this book, many people will also find themselves in situations where they are instigating change and creating change for the people around them.

An obvious example of this is in the workplace. It could be you are in a management position and making an organisational change. This may affect just one person if it is a change of role or reporting line. It may affect an entire department if it is a restructure for example. It may even impact the entire organisation in the case of new owners or new CEO with a different agenda. In a professional or business environment the focus will be on the business objectives, strategy, the new business model, and how to implement it. Much time will be given to changing the organisation. New processes will be established and new ways of working. Staff will be expected to 'embrace' the change and 'get on board'. Those that do not immediately accept the change are often considered to be negative and obstacles in the way of change. In turn their position and career is threatened.

In this environment senior leaders or managers that drive through the change aggressively are seen as strong leaders. Above all they need to deliver the new organisation. Managers are expected to implement it with their teams and departments and to quickly become fully operational. Very rarely do leaders and managers consider the personal impact to their staff beyond the obvious professional impacts. Managers are often not given the training and support needed to do so. They are equipped to conduct reviews and monitor performance, usually with a focus on those underperforming, without ever looking beneath the surface results. Many organisations will say their staff are their greatest asset. Or to be more correct, their people. By recognising and understanding the personal impact of change on people, and providing the appropriate support, an organisation can be much more effective at introducing change. This can be done in a way that keeps staff supportive and comfortable with the change. Even in the case of redundancies, recognising the life-changing event and supporting them through the change curve has enormous benefits.

It is not only in the work environment that people may be making change that impacts on others. In families, the start of new relationship, or ending of others, will often have wider ranging impacts. The desire and decision by one party to relocate, for work for example, has impacts on other members of the family. An illness or injury of a family member can have similar effects. The decisions we take will often represent a change to those closest to us, a change that has to be processed and accepted like any other. In the wider context this is also true within social groups and between friends. The same sorts of events can represent significant change to our friends.

Recognition

As with dealing with changes to our own lives we should also recognise where those we have impacted are on the change curve. We should also make the same allowances for them that we do with ourselves, for example giving people time to get over the shock/surprise before expecting them to move forward.

Where people are open with their emotions it is easier to recognise, particularly in the early stages of the change curve. Those that are more guarded will be subtle but the signs will be there. In some cases, people will simply need time but in others they will need support.

If we can recognise where people are on the change curve (and remember they may move backwards and forwards between stages), then we can manage and lead them appropriately. For example, someone in the experiment stage will be open to ideas and suggestions. The conversation can be positive and constructive. For others in the depression dip they may simply need to be given some subtle encouragement and time. Conversation about options and moving forward will be best left to another time.

Their Change, Not Yours

When implementing change, it is important to recognise that the personal change for you as an individual will be different to those around you. The two must not be confused. It may be that you are struggling with the change but your colleagues or family welcome it, and vice versa. You may have received a promotion to department manager at work, but your team have a new manager and they will have their reservations. It is the same trigger event, but the change for you is different to that of your team. Your progress through the change curve will be different to that of your team.

One important aspect of understanding the impact of change on an individual is also, if possible, to understand what other changes they are undergoing in their lives. If every other aspect is stable and positive, then it will be easier to adapt to a change in the workplace or at home. If they are also going through changes in other parts of their lives, then this new change represents additional stress that is much harder to cope with. Often responses from people in relation to an event or change are considered out of proportion with the even itself.

Ask why? It may well be there is some information you are not aware of. This may be easier to understand with close friends and family members.

Listen and Observe

Communication skill is a large topic but certain aspects are critical when leading change. When it comes to understanding the impact of change on others around us there are certain skills that particularly help.

Listen to the person you are affecting. Do not just hear the words but really listen to what they are saying. Listen to their choice of words, how they say them, what they have not said, and what lies behind their words. Listen to the intonation and the body language. Words typically make up only 7% of the communication. Particularly in the work environment people will say the 'right' thing or what they think is expected. Even with friends and family people will do the same thing or even deflect the conversation away from their true feelings. If you have any sort of responsibility to help someone through change then it is important to understand where they are on the change curve which may be different to what they are telling you.

More than what people say, actions speak louder than words. What people do and how quickly they do it will often indicate their true feelings and motivations in relation to a change situation. Procrastination and half-hearted efforts do not suggest someone is enthusiastic or accepting of change. Conversely someone pushing ahead and on top of all the actions to implement the change are clearly accepting of it. In the work or home environment, regardless of what people say, the actions they take will often give a much clearer indication of their true feelings regarding the change.

Providing Support

Every situation and person is unique. Providing the right support in a timely fashion is therefore a matter of judgment. The following tips and tools have worked for me but need to be used intelligently.

Give People Time and Space

Although the right support can help people through the change curve the pace of change cannot be forced. Depending on the scale of change and the impact people need to be given time and space to work through the curve. On occasion people simply need to be given time to work through their emotions and responses. Similarly, they need to be given the emotional 'space' to do this, i.e. to be allowed to have the feelings they have without the pressure or expectation that they should get over it and move on.

This applies to both positive and negative emotions. In a team or family environment one person may be coming out of the change curve while another is still in a period of depression. The positive emotions of the former are equally as valid as the emotions of the latter. They should also be given the space to feel these emotions and make progress through the change curve.

Be There for Them

Whatever the environment, people need to feel there is support and they are not dealing with the change completely alone. In the work environment this is recognition of the impact of change on the individual both professionally and personally. It is also recognising the individual will be going through the change curve with all the challenges and emotions that entails.

With family and friends, it is critical that if support is to be provided it is there in deed as well as word. Hollow words that are not backed up when support is requested will leave people disappointed and let down.

As you cannot force the pace of change, you also cannot force people to come to you for support. That means not being overbearing or demanding with offers of support. Simply make it known that the support is there whenever the opportunity is right.

Keep Them Informed

Depending on the scale of change and the level of impact it is much easier for people to adapt to change if they are kept informed as the change unfolds. At all stages of the change curve, and whatever the environment, people have questions regarding the change. Often these questions will go unasked. If anything that makes it all the more important that people are kept informed and given the information that will help them deal with the change.

Involve Them in Important Decisions

If possible, involving people in major decisions, rather than simply keeping them informed, will help people process the change. This gives individuals a sense of control and with this control a greater level of comfort with the change.

Above All – Integrity

When making change, and leading people through it, there is a responsibility for those people. This is not just a professional responsibility in the work environment, it is a moral responsibility at both work and at home. Those people you are leading through the change are trusting you nonetheless. They may or may not have any choice but they are trusting you. The only way to honour that trust is to operate with absolute integrity. This is a simple thing to describe and, if true to your personal values, will be simple to deliver. However, it may lead to difficult decisions or situations.

What is integrity? There are numerous definitions with variances in ethics, politics, business, and so on. These can all be stripped back to core values:

- Honesty and trust are core to integrity by any definition.
- Be true to your word. Do what you say you will do, or not do what you say you will not. This could be described as dependability, reliability, and keeping your promises.
- Be fair. Treat people fairly. Perhaps best described by what it is not. Do not discriminate or be (consciously) biased.
- Above all, operating with integrity means doing the right thing. Do the right thing for the individual, your family, your colleagues, your employer. Take care to watch out for conflicts of interest. This is where the temptation lies to do the right thing for yourself at someone else's expense.

Leading people through change, with integrity, may be simple to describe but can make some decisions and situations difficult. Doing the right thing by a team member may conflict with instructions you are given. Doing the right thing by your employer may require a personal sacrifice or compromise. However, whatever the difficulty operating with integrity will uphold the trust and confidence of the people who are relying on you. It will also keep your conscience clear.

Support for You

Leading change whether in a personal and family environment, or in a business professional environment is a significant responsibility. Not only is the success of the change dependent on leading and supporting others through it, but the personal impact of the change can have a major impact on the lives of all those involved.

There are numerous resources available to support and guide you through this process. A good starting point with my personal recommendations can be found at:
www.thekeepcalmguy.co.uk

Chapter Thirteen
Keep Calm

"Be a calm beholder of what is happening around you."
Bruce Lee

We have looked at what change is, also the change curve, and the stages we need to go through to eventually come out the other side and accept and integrate the change. We have looked at our emotional response to change and also how we can use adult rational thinking to make the best decisions. So what does keeping calm mean in the face of significant (or even small scale) change?

Firstly, we must recognise that the emotional response is natural and that it is just our inner chimp having a tantrum. But it must be allowed to have its tantrum and then be put back in its box. We can do this quickly and easily by acknowledging the emotions, but also acknowledging that they are just emotions and not our adult rational response. We cannot keep calm by ignoring the emotions or trying to use sheer will power to overcome them. Express the emotion in a safe environment and move on when you are ready to do so. This may be swearing under your breath, offloading to a close friend, or hitting the desk. Give it the time and space it deserves, but no more. At the outset remember that people move back and forward within the change curve. Emotional reactions will come and go accordingly and that is okay, it is normal, and to be expected. Just separate the emotional response from adult thinking and avoid making any significant decisions while gripped by emotion. In the face of major change you will have periods of heightened emotion, and periods of rational thinking and greater clarity.

Engage the adult brain by detaching from the situation and allowing your emotions to subside. Recognise if they have done so or if they are still bubbling under wanting more attention. Who is in control at any point the chimp or the adult? Only when the adult brain is firmly in control can you deal with the situation calmly.

At this point you can look at the situation more objectively. Consider what advice you would give others in this situation, and what advice you think others would give you. Ask for input and support if you need it from those whose judgement you respect. Look at all your options for dealing with the situation and evaluate them.

Remember the Serenity Prayer. Identify what is completely outside of your control, and what you can control or influence.

Identify what you need to act on and how quickly you need to make a decision. If you have the time, then take it to consider your options. Breaking down the change to focus on immediate priorities, and being aware of the time you have available can relieve the pressure.

Check your perspective. Are your emotions and thoughts in perspective with the change? What would others say? When you look back at the event in six months' time will your emotions and actions still seem justified? Are you looking at the situation rationally? What would others say if they were aware of your thoughts and ideas?

Think back to your own personal example or situation that will give you perspective. Having survived the London bombs on 7/7, including a pivotal moment when I did not know if I would live or die, I still have a very strong reference point to judge change events by. I can still get lost in the emotion of the moment, but thinking back this time in my life suddenly gives me a clear perspective on priorities and what is important. Obviously, most things pale into insignificance compared to this. The other benefit this gives me, is to remind myself of the inner strength I was able to find in dealing with the situation. I can remind myself that if I can deal with 7/7 I can deal with just about anything else. By putting change in this perspective the emotion subsides and I am able to deal with it.

Everyone is able to achieve the same perspective, and to acknowledge the inner strength that has enabled them to deal with other challenges. Finding the right reference point whether it is personal experience or that of close family or friends can change perspective. Looking back over past challenges and how these have been overcome can provide strength and confidence to face current ones.

Chapter Fourteen
Carry On

"Sometimes carrying on, just carrying on, is the superhuman achievement."

Albert Camus

In the hours and days that followed the 7/7 bombs I felt like I was teetering on the brink of an abyss. Looking into the abyss I could see complete denial, rejection of the world and its terrors, abdication of all my responsibilities. In short, a complete mental breakdown. The temptation to pull the duvet over my head and not come out for weeks, months, or years was very strong. It also gave me complete understanding and empathy for people that fall into the abyss – even just momentarily.

The other side of this brink was my life as I knew it. My family, my career, my plans, hopes and dreams. A normal life. Then I realised it was my decision – I could give up and just fall into the abyss, or I could turn round, face my demons, and carry on. Ultimately everyone that faces a major change, as well as the smaller ones, has to make this decision. This is the turning point, the time to carry on. For some it will be too great an ask and they will fall into the abyss. There is no shame in it, it is not a failure, just not the right time.

Carrying on is a positive choice and the point at which we start to look at the way forward. We look at our options, the actions we could take, the decisions we need to make. Emotions may still run very high, or come over us in waves, but we start to take the first steps in moving forward. Once we have taken the first step it is easier to take the second. We may not even know where our steps will lead us but my taking one step at a time we start to move forward.

This does not mean it is easy. To begin with carrying on can feel like taking steps despite not wanting to but because we know we have to. It may take all our energy and provide no satisfaction. But the second and third steps will be easier and the burden lighter. Certainly after the 7/7 bomb, but more so after losing my wife, carrying on was turning on the autopilot. The children still had to be fed, laundry still had to be done, and so on. Carrying on was a necessity.

After time we may even see the opportunities, the positive things that could or have come about as a result of the change. Even in grief families become closer and old relationships are renewed. There are always opportunities and there are always positives. They may not be obvious to begin with indeed they may not arise until months or years later. Often we need the help of others to point them out to us. At this point it is our decision to recognise them for what they are and to take the opportunity.

With the passing of time, and progression through the change curve, our lives take on a new normal. We start to accept the change and integrate it into our lives. We experiment with options and explore possibilities. We make decisions and we take control.

Looking back over the life-changing events I have experienced, and my journey through a number of change curves, there are two things that stand out. The first is the inner strength I was able to find to deal with it. But more significantly was the inner strength that I saw in other people that shared their own stories with me. I believe it is a strength that we all have but it goes untapped until we need to call on it. That is not to say that it makes dealing with the change any easier – but the strength is there and we can all find it when we need to. This inner strength is not enough in itself – we all need help and support at times in our lives. The smart thing to do is recognise this and use the help and support on offer to our advantage. It is not a failing to ask for help, it is a sign of strength and confidence.

The second thing that stands out for me is that the 'new normal' can be just as good if not better than the old one. It might take time to get there but achieving previous levels of happiness and satisfaction is perfectly possible. Following the events described in this book I have been able to rebuild my life. This new life bears very little resemblance to the old one, and is something I never would have envisaged. Dealing and coping with the change was just the first step in a long journey.

I hope this book has given you at least a few suggestions for tools and techniques for dealing with change, whether it be a major life-changing event or something more routine. Everyone is unique and the journey is a personal one. The understanding gained in this book and how I have dealt with significant events in my life has worked for me. Hopefully it will also help you to look at change events differently in the future and deal with them with more clarity and ease. To be able to keep calm in the face of change and to carry on.

One of the themes in this book is the level of control we have over our lives and the decisions we can take if we are prepared to. We have far greater control over our thinking, our feelings, our behaviours, and ultimately our lives than many believe. At each stage of the journey through the change curve we face the inner dialogue between our emotional chimp and adult brain, we face the options and possibilities for taking the next step, we face decisions. We also do not exist in isolation – we interact with others, friends, family, colleagues, etc. All of these things are aspects of dealing with the change that we can make decisions on and take control. The more that we do this the more that we are able to master the change and not be a victim of it. If we can learn to master change, then we can learn to embrace it and not fear it.